Understanding Cyber Risk

A myriad of security vulnerabilities in the software and hardware we use today can be exploited by an attacker, any attacker. The knowledge necessary to successfully intercept your data and voice links and bug your computers is widespread and not limited to the intelligence apparatus. Consequently, the knowledge required can – at least in part – also easily be accessed by criminals trying to "transfer your wealth" and competitors looking for your trade secrets. The temptation to use these easily accessible resources to the disadvantage of a rival company grows as global competition gets fiercer. Corporate espionage is nothing new, but since the dawn of the Internet age the rules have changed. It is no longer necessary to be on-site to steal proprietary information. Cyberattacks today are cheap, and attackers run a very low risk of getting caught, as attacks can be executed from anywhere in the world – an ideal breeding ground for criminal activities – and the consequences can be disastrous.

In *Understanding Cyber Risk: Protecting Your Corporate Assets*, the author provides a wealth of real-world examples from diverse industries from all over the world on how company assets are attacked via the cyber world. The cases clearly show that any organisation can fall victim to a cyberattack, regardless of size or country of origin. He also offers specific advice on how to protect core assets and company secrets.

This book is essential reading for anyone interested in cybersecurity and the use of cyberattacks in corporate espionage.

Thomas R. Koehler is a founding director of CE21 Consulting, which provides specialist consultancy support to clients throughout Europe, including major telecommunications providers, medium and large enterprises of various industries, government bodies and international organisations. Before founding CE21 in 2007, he worked as a research assistant at the University of Würzburg and subsequently launched two successful start-ups in the dawning of the Internet era. He is also on the supervisory board of Baliqa Invest AG, a company focusing on technology investments. Thomas is the author of several books highlighting the risks and opportunities of our connected world for both individuals and businesses. He is a regular media commentator on Internet and society and has appeared on television and radio.

Understanding Cyber Risk

Protecting Your Corporate Assets

Thomas R. Koehler

Routledge
Taylor & Francis Group

LONDON AND NEW YORK

First published 2018
by Routledge

2 Park Square, Milton Park, Abingdon, Oxfordshire OX14 4RN
52 Vanderbilt Avenue, New York, NY 10017

Routledge is an imprint of the Taylor & Francis Group, an informa business

First issued in paperback 2020

British Library Cataloguing-in-Publication Data
A catalogue record for this book is available from the British Library

Library of Congress Cataloging-in-Publication Data
Names: Koehler, Thomas R., 1968– author.
Title: Understanding cyber risk : protecting your corporate assets / Thomas
    R. Koehler.
Description: Abingdon, Oxon ; New York, NY : Routledge, 2018. |
    Includes bibliographical references and index.
Identifiers: LCCN 2017032211 | ISBN 9781472477798 (hardback) |
    ISBN 9781315549248 (ebook)
Subjects: LCSH: Data protection. | Business intelligence. | Business
    enterprises—Computer networks—Security measures. | Computer
    crimes—Prevention.
Classification: LCC HF5548.37 .K64 2018 | DDC 658.4/78—dc23
LC record available at https://lccn.loc.gov/2017032211

ISBN: 978-1-4724-7779-8 (hbk)
ISBN: 978-0-367-60592-6 (pbk)

Typeset in Bembo
by Apex CoVantage, LLC

Contents

Foreword

Only the paranoid survive.

Andy Grove, former head of Intel

I remember precisely that it was a Wednesday morning, even if I can no longer remember the precise date. It was the beginning of the 1990s, I was a student and the holidays had just begun. Unlike my fellow students, I was not down at the beach but in a large mechanical engineering company in Southern Germany. Six weeks' work in the factory during the summer break helped me to finance my degree. I was already familiar with the company and the work, but I just couldn't get used to getting up so early – work always started at 7 a.m. At least this summer I had managed to secure myself one of the sought-after jobs looking after visitors. That meant giving up all kinds of supplementary payments – and ultimately less money – but pleasant working conditions, including extended lunch breaks in a cafeteria known as the Casino which was really reserved for management and their visitors.

All that I had to do was to pick up visitors – always in groups of at least two – and to accompany them through various stations consisting of design, production and logistics according to a predetermined schedule and to bring them to lunch and coffee. Often, I had the opportunity to learn something or other about company processes: at each station in the factory, the responsible person would give a short presentation on what was particularly interesting about the process being demonstrated according to a precise plan. Unfortunately, just about all that I can remember is the amusing English used in the style of "we can do everything except speak decent English".

Then, that Wednesday, I had what was to become my own personal defining moment, which caused me to explore in depth the topic of economically motivated espionage – a topic which will accompany me for the rest of my professional life and which has now resulted in this book, a quarter of a century after the event.

We arrived in the canteen at lunchtime as always – but one seat at the festively decorated table remained empty. One of the guests was missing, but it was impossible to tell which of the group of Asians in dark suits and white shirts it was. They all dressed too alike for both me and the colleague with whom I was sharing the task. Because we couldn't tell them apart we hadn't noticed the loss of a member of the group until that moment. A head count confirmed our suspicions: the table was laid correctly but one participant, who was still present when the visitors' passes were issued in the morning, had now vanished – a case for the works security people. Half an hour later, after an orchestrated search action across the entire campus, he was discovered in a copying room in the main building, far away from the route taken by the group. Apparently he had taken a particular fancy to a folder of design plans from a supervisor's office on a new production line. He was carrying this along with a few photocopies – he had taken a targeted approach and had been very selective with copying material.

However, what happened after that completely amazed me: unexpectedly, there was no big fuss at all. The renegade visitor was escorted back to the group by the works security people, lunch was taken together somewhat late, and the visitors' programme in the afternoon continued as planned – with slightly shorter presentations. The main difference that afternoon was that in addition to my colleague and me, four members of the works security were always inconspicuously in the vicinity of the group until they departed – as inconspicuously as is possible in a black uniform and with a walkie-talkie attached to your trouser belt.

But basically, nothing happened: nobody phoned the police, nor was the incident itself made litigable. Quite the opposite: a great effort was made to prevent anything getting out and to save face in front of the visitors. It was only years later that I understood why the company not only had done nothing in the face of such an obvious case of attempted theft of know-how but also had done everything possible to cover up the incident: nobody wanted to do anything which could jeopardise a planned joint venture in China.

Today, almost 25 years later, a lot has changed at the mechanical engineering company. After numerous ups and downs, it is now prospering as part of a large German corporation, and information processing and communication technology within the company have developed dramatically – so much further that today talk is often of extensive digitalisation or a digital transformation. It may also be that the attempted know-how theft which I experienced would no longer need a photocopier but would make use of the new possibilities which the extensive networking of our society with Internet and smartphones brings with it.

Soundlessly and without causing any commotion, but effective: this is indeed a good description of the new methods of what is generally known as industrial espionage. This book traces the new, dangerous and partly unbelievable methods by means of several concrete examples – not as instructions to be copied but as a warning and to protect the companies affected against the acute espionage risks of the 21st century. It also covers additional risks that come with the new technical capabilities of the attackers, which includes sabotage, as well as theft of intangible assets and other crimes, that can be committed conveniently via the Internet. Organisations of all sizes are at risk – from individual entrepreneurs to multinational concerns.

Thomas R. Koehler
Munich, November 2017

1 Espionage

An underestimated matter

It is part of human nature to inadequately assess risks. Whole groups of hazards are systematically underestimated and others greatly overestimated. A prime example of an overestimated threat is the perception of the risk involved in being injured by a shark. The threat appears enormous and the summer headlines of large popular newspapers cannot be imagined without reports of shark attacks.

On looking closely, however, it becomes apparent that only 70 to 100 shark attacks take place per year worldwide with 5 to 15 deaths. This semi-official documentation of such incidents by the International Shark Attack File (ISAF) of the University of Florida supplies the hard facts (ISAF 2016). Whether and how many British or American nationals are injured by shark attacks is not known in detail. But it can safely be assumed that at least the Brits are rather underrepresented since sharks do not normally occur along British coastlines.

If the fear of sharks was regarded as rational and consequently used as a measure of risks to life, one would rather have cause to worry about choking on swallowed food at every meal; 615 people died in such a manner in Germany – a country with a population of 80 million people – in one year alone (CHOKE 2010). However, nothing is known of the existence of huge fears within large sections of the population of having an accident during meals.

Human fears and worries are seldom rational. The risk of being run over whilst popping down to the bakers' shop before breakfast is probably higher than becoming a shark victim whilst on holiday. The risk of becoming a victim of identity theft online is also seriously higher – whereby it is hardly possible for people to estimate such "invisible" risks. At least with the shark, we have a graphic picture of the danger in our mind's eye ever since *Jaws* came out.

Generations of psychologists have already considered the question of why people who otherwise behave extremely prosaically and are very statistically focussed react so irrationally when assessing risks. Researchers at the University of Dartmouth and other behavioural scientists see our subconscious at work here and point out the proven usefulness of our intuitive assessment of risks in former millennia, which consequently also leads to diffuse fears of hazards caused by humans. It's just too bad that our modern world has so far been too ephemeral to change perceptions shaped over a long period of time.

It is not only we as private persons who are confronted with the problem of an inadequate ability for assessing risks but also equally responsible persons in companies. Perception is often the cause of worries specifically in the field of company security. The same goes for carelessness. IT security specialists know a thing or two about that. Regardless of whether it's down to the head of IT or the company security department or even management itself, the job of being responsible for computer security is regarded, not without reason, as one of the most thankless tasks within a company – a view which I found confirmed time and again during the years I worked on building up secure IT and telecommunications infrastructures. No praise is to be expected because it is taken for granted that everything should work as it should. If something goes wrong and a security-related incident happens, the head of security is held responsible – and can sometimes find themselves looking for another job.

Even in "times of peace" the task is not a trivial one, as resources for necessary investments in security products are often not regarded as being especially important by management; after all, no return on investment (RoI) can be calculated here. This RoI is a key income figure which denotes the economic success of an investment measure. At first glance, calculating an RoI appears to be a good idea here, but with investments in company security the RoI is inappropriate because at best the result of this key figure is future savings – if everything goes well. Due to this dilemma, only a few companies are as well positioned regarding security as they should be.

Yesterday's paranoia is tomorrow's threat

It took the revelations of Edward Snowden about the activities of the US National Security Agency (NSA) and the British Government Communications Headquarters (GCHQ) and the media's indignation about German chancellor Angela Merkel's mobile phone being bugged to create awareness amongst the general public for one of the most important issues of our age: espionage. However, the fact that national intelligence services also spy on "friendly countries" is the wrong reason for the public debate because we can safely assume that it is the task of any intelligence service to know the political state of its own allies. But it is also the task of the counterintelligence of any given country to keep the other side's spies at arm's length. Awkward intimacies between the services – as they have come to light in the course of the revelations – should be prohibited as a matter of course.

What is really worrying about the documents published by Edward Snowden from 2013 on is the large amount of detailed technical information which shows the vulnerability of our economic and social exchanges based on information and telecommunications to unauthorised access by third parties.

The same applies to the information about the US Central Intelligence Agency (CIA) hacking targets published years later – in 2017. The latter even included TVs and cars. One concrete example showed how to use a Samsung TV as an audio bug by updating its firmware so that the attacker could listen to everything that was spoken in this room. In this case the software even allowed one to switch the power indicator of the TV to off so nobody would take notice. Since TV usage is not limited to the private setting of your living room, and TVs can be found in hotel rooms, lobbies, bars and conference centres, the potential reach of this attack vector is larger than one might think at first.

Following these revelations, in February 2017, security research from Swiss security consulting company Oneconsult presented a way to remotely take over smart TVs by manipulating the broadcast signal to the European Broadcasting Union. As Oneconsult found out, more than 90 percent of all smart TVs are vulnerable to these kinds of attacks.

In 2015 security researchers managed to hack a Fiat Chrysler Grand Cherokee SUV via the remote connectivity option of its Uconnect infotainment system. The attackers were able to control the brakes, disengage the transmission and change the settings of the climate controls as well as the radio stations. Fiat Chrysler fixed the vulnerability with a security patch after the story went public and made big headlines. The patch needs to be installed at the dealer or via a USB drive – there is no way to update the car over the air so one should expect that a high percentage of the Grand Cherokee cars with this special version of the Uconnect infotainment system currently on the road are still vulnerable to the very same attack. It is not known whether the attack would allow eavesdropping on the conversations between the driver and the passengers via the built-in microphone of the hands-free module included in Uconnect, but one should expect so, since the researcher successfully gained access to several critical vehicle functions. Your car is also at risk of being hijacked if you do not own a car equipped with Uconnect. Several aftermarket dongles that attach to the OBD-2 port, which is standard in all cars built since the 1990s, are also vulnerable to access. These dongles typically allow vehicle tracking or fleet management functions to be added to cars. Since they connect to the main data bus in the car (the CAN bus) they also potentially can be used to hack the vehicle in similar ways to those shown with Fiat Chrysler. Consequently researches found a security hole in a dongle provided by Bosch for their fleet management solution, which can be exploited via Bluetooth, which means you have to be nearby (e.g. following the car with another car). Bosch already provided a security update for this problem, but the next vulnerability is just around the corner.

Of course, these are just examples. But hopefully they will open our eyes to an unbelievable variety of technical aids and processes which permit individuals and companies to be spied on and which we can assume the use of which is not limited to the intelligence services.

If one deals with the security of organisations professionally, one is not infrequently suspected of being a doomsayer and conspiracy theorist oneself. The revelations on the machinations of the intelligence services have, above all, achieved one thing, namely bringing things out into the open which have long been discussed in specialist circles – for example the possibility of building back doors into hardware and software. Whether smartphones, drones or autonomous vehicles, every new development brings new possibilities but also new security risks. In addition, new security holes are discovered in technologies already in use every day. The question as to the security situation of an organisation or a company must therefore be asked anew every day.

In a discussion on technical security, the topic has by now developed into such an important one that there is a tendency to differentiate between a time before and a time after Snowden. As a security expert, you are no longer automatically regarded as the weirdo that you were put down as until recently but are suddenly being listened to – at least occasionally. And just as the "Snowden effect" begins to wear down, new revelations add fuel to the flames. Regarding this development neutrally and without emotion, it must be said that yesterday's paranoia has become tomorrow's security threat.

Digital transformation and espionage

Whether we like it or not, we are all in the middle of a huge transformation, the scope of which can only be compared to the Industrial Revolution. The consensus is that so-called digital transformation has changed our lives and the way we work in the second decade of the 21st century. In just a few decades, almost everything to do with private and professional communication has changed.

The beginnings were fairly unspectacular: in the mid-1990s, the Internet wave washed over the edge of the academic world and initially conquered technically oriented parts of the population. "Are you connected?", a phrase from an advert for an online service provider, became a familiar expression. But the Internet has long ceased just to be the playground of a few technology freaks. A business card without an email address has now become just as unimaginable as a company without a website – the Internet has become a fixed part of our lives and working environment.

Official figures speak a clear language. From data provided by the Office of National Statistics (ONS), 87.9 percent of adults in the United Kingdom (45.9 million) had recently (within a three-month time frame) used the Internet (ONS 2016). The Internet penetration rate of the United States in 2016 is up to similar levels: 88.5 percent (LIVESTAT 2016). Comparable numbers exist throughout the developed world. Equally impressive is the time spent using the Internet. Typically it adds up to several hours a day, especially for younger users.

The penetration of mobile phone connections is significantly above 100 percent in the Western world. Even more important is that most mobile phone users are smartphone users now. UK numbers for 2016 show that more than 80 percent of all mobile phone users are smartphone users. A press release by Ofcom – the United Kingdom's national communication regulator – in 2015 mentioned an important point of inflection. At that time, the primary means of Internet access changed from the PC to the smartphone. Thanks to Internet and mobile phones we are always online nowadays – always in contact.

The so-called smartphone has had a major share in increasing online use in private and professional life in recent years. Mobile phone technology was first introduced in the summer of 1992 as the so-called D network based on the widespread Global System for Mobile Communication (GSM) standard and was consequently affordable for everyone. Since then, the mobile phone has experienced unprecedented success. In 2002, there were already more mobile phones worldwide than fixed-line phone connections according to the International Telecommunication Union (ITU), and since 2006, the ITU has even observed a reduction in the number of fixed-land phone connections.

The relatively young category of smartphones is playing a special role in this as their prevalence and use are growing rapidly. According to figures by Gartner, a market research institute, around 1.5 billion units were sold in 2016 alone. Beyond telephone functionality, smartphone users have the option of sending and receiving e-mails, using further Internet services and installing applications like on a computer. These programmes, known as apps, not only provide functions for casual users, from video games to fitness trackers, torches to navigation systems, but also increasingly provide business applications such as access to company-specific software, internal company calendars and other company databases.

The smartphone became a success story with the advent of the iPhone, which was introduced by Apple in 2007. Its intuitive operation via touchscreen – and later also voice control – facilitated the breakthrough of the concept of the mobile phone with added value and thus also mobile Internet use. The Android operating system initiated by Google started up in its wake and became a global success – thanks to the support of many manufacturers. The device type was complemented by tablets, which started their triumphal march initially in private households and are meanwhile also indispensable in professional life.

Access to company data is clearly at the forefront of benefit models – even if a lot of "business" iPads meanwhile seen in trains and airport lounges are rather being used for online games or videos. In practise, business and private use intermingle with this very personal piece of technology – whether smartphone or tablet – something which will play an important role in the course of this book.

Security risks included

If the promises of IT providers are to be believed, every company which is mainly controlled from on the road and the home office becomes a mobile enterprise. The omnipresent connection via Internet and mobile telecommunications permits the dissolution of the spatial limits of what used to be a company campus. Some companies already only exist as so-called virtual organisations, which de facto consist of a network, the ends of which are determined by the respective locations of the employees – and these can also just as well be a coffee shop, an intercity train or an airport lounge.

However, this beautiful new world of work is potentially also a beautiful new world of espionage. Why smuggle in an extra employee to secretly copy important design documents when an attack "from the comfort of your own home" via the Internet is much easier? Thinking the possibilities of these new worlds of communication through to the end, it is possible to imagine totally new patterns of attack which presumably have already been tried, for the main lesson of technical history so far is that everything that can be done has been done.

The core problem of our current situation is simple: the standardised Internet-based processes for communication, so-called Internet protocols, are not designed for secure communication. The popular notion that an e-mail is as secure against being read by unwanted eyes as a postcard is not just idle talk. In fact, things are even worse: you can't even trust the sender. There are e-mail encryption processes, but they are so complex to use their acceptance in private life and in business is low. People have simply come to accept the situation and sometimes bypass the problem by at least sending the attachment in encrypted form.

The same applies to using the World Wide Web for transactions: there are additional security mechanisms but until recently they were extremely problematic to implement from a technical point of view. A vulnerability in OpenSSL, which was christened "Heartbleed", which could crack open the encryption of Internet connections important for e-commerce in many application cases, was discovered in April 2014 (OPENSSL 2014). The most shocking thing was that it was a programming error by one single developer in an open source project which had caused this dangerous security vulnerability. Nobody had checked the programme code – but the software was deployed many times. In the end, the error remained undiscovered for more than two years. The statistics provider Netcraft assumes that half a million websites were affected by this error (NETCRAFT 2014).

It should also not be forgotten that no guarantees of quality and availability are given for normal use of the Internet, that is to say, without any additional technical measures. An expert calls this "best effort", meaning that if it works it works and that you just have to put up with it if it only works slowly and maybe even not at all for certain applications. But what if a competitor decides to slow down your company communication to such an extent that it is impossible to work? You think something like that never happens and that it's just a theoretical problem? Unfortunately, the reality of the 21st century is different.

The inadequacies of the Internet infrastructure are so great that researchers are seriously considering starting again from scratch and redeveloping it – with built-in security features. But the chances of this clean-slate approach being realised appear to be minimal – the power of the installed base is too great. Security within mobile phone networks is also lagging a long way behind what is technically possible. Here, however, the starting conditions are different: the GSM standard and the encryption used are less secure than they could have been when they were introduced. State intelligence services allegedly had an influence on them – a fact which I have had confirmed to me by a former high-level GSM standard developer.

Added to this are further security risks. Even though Linux and Mac OS do crop up occasionally, our computer landscape is dominated by Microsoft operating systems. Similar to monocultures in agriculture and forestry, this makes structures especially susceptible to infestation. As a result, we have had a dramatic increase in the incidence of computer infestations such as viruses, worms and Trojans along-side the rise of the Internet. Although malware for computers is by no means an invention of the network age, in the past the main means of distribution was limited to floppy disks. This meant that the means and speed of distribution of an infection were severely limited, whereas nowadays, in extreme cases, thousands of computers can be infected with a new security threat within just a few hours.

There is less of a monoculture with smartphones. Regarding distribution, Google's Android operating system, which is deployed by a wide number of manufacturers, dominates here. The big problem with this is the almost uncontrollable growth of different devices with different Android variants and version numbers. The result is that most devices on the market receive either inadequate updates or none at all. The official numbers speak for themselves: as reported by the Google Security blog in early 2017, almost half of all Android devices did not receive a security update in 2016. Security vulnerabilities therefore often remain unsolved.

At this point, those who now ask themselves what the purpose of updates for mobile phones is because we used to get by without them should remember this: today, mobile phones are no longer mobile phones in the original sense but basically computers, some of which have the same performance as some computers had just a few years ago and which are permanently connected to the Internet via the mobile phone network – a worthwhile target of attack from a hacker's point of view. It is therefore no wonder that the malware emerging for smartphones, especially for ones with an Android operating system, has positively exploded in recent years.

That would not be so bad if the use of these devices was limited to our private lives. But in fact, many of these private devices find their way into companies, where they are suddenly being used for company business by way of modern "bring your own device" (BYOD) concepts – and sometimes even in addition to official company smartphones, with which occasional private use can hardly be prevented. Uncontrolled communication via BYOD and private end devices additionally increases the vulnerability of the company in the face of both targeted and nondirectional attacks.

There are voices at this point which call for the abolition of smartphone and network access. But that is not practicable in day-to-day business, which mainly consists of trade relationships with suppliers and customers. In short, in business life, we are thoroughly dependent on technology. We must reconcile ourselves to this regardless of how we assess the further development of the associated risks. In order not to fall into a state of shock in the face of the putative "killer shark", it is high time that we turned our attention to the challenges which the Internet age brings for the security of our companies against information drains, sabotage and other damage to competitiveness and survivability in detail.

Technical progress

With all the experience with digital change that we already have, it is easy to understand that more networking brings new security risks with it. The fact that the further development of well-known technologies means new hazards emerge and old ones have to be reassessed is often overlooked.

One example of this is, of all things, a technology which is already hundreds of years old: the door lock with its mechanical key, which is practically the same everywhere. Both burglars and spies have always been in a race with lock manufacturers for security and access protection. For years, the media have been complaining about the unlimited sale of tools for committing burglary with the argument that their availability increases the risk of being burgled for the general population. Tools for lock picking, as the opening of locks without using a key is known, are freely available on large Internet marketplaces. But these sets of skeleton keys, as they are traditionally called, are of little use to ordinary people; some instruction and a lot of practise are required to overcome even the simplest locking mechanisms. It is possible to teach oneself the necessary skills with an instruction manual and YouTube videos, but it is also possible to join an association such as the "Sportsfreunde der Sperrtechnik" (Sports Fans of Locking Technology), who explain the purpose of the association on their website as follows (SST 2017):

> The maintenance of locking technology as a sporting challenge. For us, the term locking technology means all processes and knowledge which limit access by mean of mechanical and/or electronic measures (locks, locking systems and other security technology).

The association expressly distances itself from all illegal activities. But due to standard tools and instructions, those who want to get by without expending too much effort or joining such a club have a good chance of getting the better of a lot of locks. Lock picking as a competitive sport is nothing new. As historians point out there is proof that lock-picking competitions were pretty common in mid-Victorian-era Britain: "Lock-picking contests played a significant role in the commodification of security and the emergence of the security industry in the 1850s and 1860s", says David Churchill, lecturer in criminal justice at the University of Leeds (Churchill 2015). But now the necessary knowledge is no longer arcane but rather freely available to all via the Internet.

But there are other alternatives, for technical progress doesn't stop at the venerable technology of the mechanical door lock. The Key.me start up in the United States can help: it just takes a mobile phone photo of the key with the practical iPhone app and the automatically made replacement keys can be picked up from a kind of Mister Minit machine a few minutes later – custom made and with a guarantee. The company's target market and that of similar providers is of course not burglars and information thieves but private citizens and the owners of small companies who wish to deposit a kind of electronic version of their keys with Key.me in case they lose their keys or lock themselves out (Greenberg 2014). Put another way, burglary and espionage in offices and hotel rooms? There's an app for that: a mobile phone picture of the keys suffices, and Key.me deals with everything else for the amateur spy. For those for whom this is not enough, with suitable camera technology it may also be possible under some circumstances to photograph the key in acceptable quality from a distance – for example whilst it is being held by the legitimate owner.

Of course, this solution is just one example of the increasing general accessibility and ever-improving usability of knowledge and tools which can be used to spy on the competition. However, when analysing the security level of companies with regard to possible back doors for spies, it is worth keeping an eye on not only electronic media but also classical access routes and changes in conventional technology, for security risks are lurking everywhere.

Loss is everywhere

The Ponemon Institute, a consulting company specialising in information security, made headlines in 2008 with the results of a study. This investigated the question of how many notebooks are lost every year in American airports and how many are recovered (Bialik 2008). The figures were alarming. According to the study, more than 12,000 notebooks disappear in American airports every week – that is to say, they are stolen or lost. There are no comparable figures for Europe, but we can assume that the order of magnitude is about the same. What is especially problematic is that only a small proportion of the notebooks, some 35 percent, are protected against unauthorised access to the company data they contain, for example with suitable encryption mechanisms, and only 48 percent of those interviewed had a backup of the data on the notebook.

This is especially serious in view of the fact that around half of the notebooks investigated contain confidential business information or customer data and at least 14 percent contain data which can be regarded as business secrets, for example programme code, CAD drawings and the like. Add to this the fact that two thirds of these lost, forgotten or stolen notebooks are never recovered and the extent of the problem becomes clear.

According to an investigation commissioned by Intel in 2009, the loss of a notebook costs a company on average almost US$50,000 – for every single computer (Maisto 2009). And only around 3 percent of that goes toward replacing hardware and software. What the figures look like in Europe is uncertain. However, I know of several German companies where around 10 percent of their stocks of notebooks are lost or stolen every year. The question remains as to why companies so rarely take security measures to limit the consequences of a not-so-unlikely theft a little.

What targets a thief pursues in practise is almost impossible to comprehend in individual cases. But we can assume that notebook thefts in airports and railway stations, in conference centres and other locations frequented by businesspeople are often deliberately targeted because there is a possibility of obtaining promising stocks of data.

I have not yet lost a computer, but I have been the target of attempted thefts several times: once, a fellow traveller tried to fish my (password-protected) smartphone out of its case on the conveyor at the security check-in at Munich airport, and on another occasion my notebook (protected by hard disk encryption) was about to walk off without me from the conference room in a hotel at Frankfurt Airport. Fortunately, my alertness spared me any real loss in both cases. It is especially strange that both incidents happened right under the noses of security people who claimed to have seen nothing. The perpetrators in both cases tried to get away with claiming it was an accident.

Smartphones have experienced a similar development in regards to loss figures: already in 2005, 63,000 mobile phones and almost 5,000 notebooks were allegedly left behind in London taxi cabs (Leyden 2005). Such large figures can doubtless be discounted, but the loss of end devices with company data stored on them is still a high risk, regardless of whether they are smartphones or notebooks or tablets.

Why we hear so little about industrial espionage

According to the Brookings Institute, an US think tank, over 65 percent of most companies' value, sources of revenue and growth lie in information assets, intellectual property (IP) and proprietary competitive advantages.

No wonder these values are under attack. The US Commerce Department estimates that the annual loss attributed to intellectual property theft topped US$250 billion for businesses in the United States in 2010, which translates to at least 750,000 job losses in the same period. Furthermore the International Chamber of Commerce sees the global fiscal loss due to intellectual property theft to be at least US$600 billion per year, while a study conducted by the British Broadcasting Company (BBC) comes to the conclusion that global damages in industrial espionage exceeded US$300 billion per year. The British MI5 security agency estimates the losses for British corporations due to spying to be as high as US$16 billion annually, with a single incident alone costing a UK company roughly US$1.2 billion.

For Canada, the Canadian Security and Intelligence Services (CSIS) estimate the losses for Canadian businesses between US$50–$150 billion a year in 2011. Australian officials report US$3 billion a year. The Federation of German Industry (BDI) assumes some €50 billion and the Association of German Engineers (VDI) at least €100 billion for Germany. For Austria, Corporate Trust estimates annual losses of €1.6 billion, although here too there are differing estimates. About 27 percent of all companies in Germany and Austria suffered a concrete case of espionage over a two-year time frame according to investigations by the Corporate Trust consulting company in 2014 (Trust 2014). More than 20 percent had at least reasonable suspicion. But according to official police statistics in Germany, this translates to "just" 5,500 to 7,000 cases reported every year, where they appear under the headings of "competitor offences" and "spying on data" (BKA 2016).

Despite the numbers, media reports on such incidents are extremely thin on the ground. Usually, the public only hears something if a perpetrator is actually put on trial or is sentenced – something which happens very rarely.

From a company's point of view, there are good reasons why reports on industrial espionage only rarely become public. To admit that you have been a victim of industrial espionage makes a company appear vulnerable. A reputation as an easy target may be seen by other "interested parties" as an open invitation to attack the company. Such public relations are also not terribly beneficial for a company's reputation with business partners and customers, and for companies which obtain finance from the capital market, such an incident can impair their stock market price – which top managers, whose bonuses rely on precisely this stock market price, don't want to risk. The result is that even if – or especially if – the company's own employees are involved, a silent departure from the company for them is preferable to a court case, which would mean unwelcome public attention. Due to my professional commitment I have come to the conclusion that security incidents which indicate espionage are often swept under the carpet in the IT department or by those responsible for security – after all, these people want to keep their jobs.

Similar numbers can be found for other countries. In a survey conducted by the FBI, half of the 165 private US companies that participated have claimed to be victims of economic espionage or theft of trade secrets, and 95 percent of those attempts originated from individuals associated with the Chinese government (Bruer 2015)

The danger is therefore very real – and there are a large number of companies affected. However, in the course of my research only a few companies were prepared to open up for this book. Even if a guarantee that security-relevant incidents would be presented anonymously was given, many responsible managers did not want to give any information as to whether and in what form they had become victims of such machinations. Even in cases which cannot be easily denied due to more or less extensive media coverage, the information which is given out is sparse. Nevertheless, in the course of research it has been possible to bring together a large number of cases and to analyse their backgrounds.

Ultimately, only an obligation to publish reports defined by legislature will be able to break through this wall of silence. Such legislation is due to be introduced in most countries.

2 From competition to economic warfare

Globalisation intensifies competition. That's a platitude, but a platitude with unwanted side effects, for competition is not always the same as fair dealings. This applies particularly in situations where companies have a technological head start or can simply sell cheaper. Here, the inferiority of a market participator sometimes leads to the members of its management resorting to unfair methods when trying to extend and secure their own positions. Frequently, the competitor appears to be barely tangible and rather an abstract entity at the other end of the world. All inhibitions are then quickly dropped. Cultural perceptions of what constitutes fair competition are also not identical all over the world. From this initial situation it is often just a small step to what would be regarded as an act of war elsewhere.

Business means war

War is often spoken about in the business world when it is a matter of competition between companies. The language in companies and economic media is full of war metaphors: managers are neutralised, the sales department is brought into position, then it's off to the front, no prisoners will be taken and maybe finally the pipe of peace will be smoked. If war means the absence of peace, it can definitely be concluded that the economy is a special kind of war.

In any case, management theorists and strategists like to draw on the theories of Niccolò Machiavelli (*Dell'Arte della Guerra*) and Carl von Clausewitz (*Vom Kriege*), whose chronicles from the 16th and 19th centuries continue to have an effect today and which are echoed comprehensively in management literature. However, many company managers rather seem to be inspired by works which are a great deal older and also do not originate from Western culture: we are speaking about *The Art of War* by Sunzi, also spelt Sun Tzu (Tzu no date a). The 13 chapters of the "war philosopher's" work from the 6th and 5th century BC are regarded as the oldest book on strategy. It can be condensed down to half a dozen main aspects which lead to military success (Tzu no date b).

1   The good cause. Every leader must go to war for a good cause; otherwise the troops are not properly motivated.
2   Leadership. The leader must be wise and courageous, but also strict and benevolent; otherwise his troops won't follow him.

3   Environmental conditions. When planning, it is important always to be aware of environmental conditions. Changes in them can thwart even the best of plans.

4   Terrain. The commander must familiarise himself with the terrain; otherwise his troops will fall prey to surprise attacks.

5   Organisation and discipline. In order to gain the upper hand in a military confrontation and to avoid chaos, the troops must be well organised and disciplined.

6   Espionage. Sun Tzu explains the various kinds of spies and their deployment (locals, insiders, double agents, moribund and alive). Without spies, it is impossible to obtain reliable information and knowledge about your opponent. For "when you know the enemy and yourself, you don't need to worry about the outcome of a hundred battles".

Sunzi regarded espionage as being very important. The original text contains a separate chapter on the topic which is still worth reading today, 2,500 years later, in order to understand the phenomenon of spying on competitors in the rough reality of global competition. Sunzi regards "prior knowledge" as something central and is enlightened enough to state that it is just as impossible to coax it out of ghosts as it is from experience and inference. As regards the enemy's plans, they can only be determined through spies. Here he differentiates between five classes: native spies, internal spies, defected spies, moribund spies and surviving spies. Sunzi regards the highest sanctification of his strategy to have been reached if all five types are being deployed: native spies are inhabitants of an area whose help one secures with friendly treatment. Officials of the enemy's who have been degraded, punished or passed over when posts are distributed or who are greedy for gold are regarded as internal spies (Tzu no date c):

> In this way you will be able to ascertain the condition of the hostile country and learn of plans being made against you; and you can also disturb the harmony and drive a wedge between the ruler and his ministers. But extreme care is required when dealing with internal spies.

As with spies who have defected from the enemy, these can be lured with large sums of money and promises. Sunzi also does not shrink from deliberately sacrificing people; his moribund spies serve to distribute misinformation and to deliberately fool the opponent about attack plans. That these are perhaps subsequently sentenced to death is a risk he is prepared to take. Surviving spies serve to bring back information from the enemy's camp. This is the usual class of spy which is essential to any army (Tzu no date c):

> Your surviving spy must be a man of outstanding intellect but with the outward appearance of a fool; of shabby appearance but with an iron will. He must be dynamic, resilient, strong and courageous; thoroughly used to all kinds of dirty work, able to bear hunger and cold and to incur shame and opprobrium.

Before he finishes, Sunzi goes into the management and control of espionage and points out how discretely and confidentially relations with spies should be treated and how well they should be rewarded.

The following examples clearly show that very little has changed in human terms and in relation to motivation in the last 2,500 years when it comes to gaining knowledge of your opponent's or competitor's plans. However, so much has changed in recent decades from a technological point of view, especially since the advent of universal networking via Internet and mobile communications, that it can safely be assumed that the main rules of the game have also changed – above all in the struggle for the best information about opponents and their plans.

The great confusion of terms and definitions

The discussion about spying on information turns up a large variety of terms which are not immediately understandable and not always used unequivocally: industrial espionage, economic espionage and spying on the competition are the most common terms.

A good definition of industrial espionage can be found on Investopedia (Investopedia 2017):

> Industrial espionage is the theft of trade secrets by the removal, copying or recording of confidential or valuable information in a company for use by a competitor. Industrial espionage is conducted for commercial purposes rather than national security purposes (espionage), and should be differentiated from competitive intelligence, which is the legal gathering of information by examining corporate publications, websites, patent filings and the like, to determine a corporation's activities.
>
> Industrial espionage describes covert activities, such as the theft of trade secrets, bribery, blackmail and technological surveillance. Industrial espionage is most commonly associated with technology-heavy industries, particularly the computer and auto sectors, in which a significant amount of money is spent on research and development (R&D).

In contrast, the definition of economic espionage is broader, as provided by Cornell University Law School (Cornell n.d. a):

> In general terms, economic espionage is the unlawful or clandestine targeting or acquisition of sensitive financial, trade or economic policy information; proprietary economic information; or technological information.

Typically economic espionage includes state actors, as opposed to industrial espionage and spying on the competition.

For the companies affected it is irrelevant where the threat comes from. Rather, it is quite the opposite: if the competition gets hold of the company's own business secrets it is simply irrelevant how they got there. The potential for damage is identical in both cases. A further important argument against this breakdown is that due to the use of Internet and mobile phone technology which dominates the online age for attacking companies – which is the main focus of this book – it is difficult or impossible to differentiate between cyberespionage activities which originate indirectly from a foreign intelligence service and those coming directly from a competitor or even those that even serve to prepare for other criminal activities and thus strictly speaking do not fall within the definition of espionage. "Cyber espionage describes the stealing of secrets stored in digital formats or on computers and IT networks" (FT 2012).

Most countries in the world have outlawed espionage. More than 20 years ago the US Congress officially instated the Economic Espionage Act (EEA), which became a kind of prototype for lawmakers around the world.

The EEA outlaws two forms of trade secret theft: theft for the benefit of a foreign entity (economic espionage) and theft for pecuniary gain (theft of trade secrets). It is important to note that its reach extends to theft from electronic storage. Offenders face lengthy prison terms (up to 15 years for economic espionage and up to 10 years for theft of trade secrets) as well as heavy fines (up to US$250,000 for individuals and US$5 million for organisations), and they must pay restitution.

According to the Economic Espionage Act from 1996, trade secrets include (Cornell n.d. b)

> all forms and types of financial, business, scientific, technical, economic, or engineering information, including patterns, plans, compilations, program devices, formulas, designs, prototypes, methods, techniques, processes, procedures, programs, or codes, whether tangible or intangible, and whether or how stored, compiled, or memorialized physically, electronically, graphically, photographically, or in writing.

However, laws do not always help when it comes to fighting corporate or industrial espionage, especially if the offenders are located in other countries and commit their crimes remotely via the Internet and other networks.

Whenever economic or industrial espionage are mentioned in this book, the broadest possible definition is used, with good reason. This means that no differentiation is initially made as to whether it is a matter of state-controlled or private industrial attacks. In provable individual cases, a selection is made according to the origin and motivation of the attacks. Regardless of the respective term used for activities at the expense of companies, this book mainly examines developments from the point of view of those affected.

When dealing with competition analysis and espionage, a number of technical terms and acronyms crop up which are not normally used elsewhere, namely OSINT, HUMINT and SIGINT:

> OSINT. In intelligence service slang, this stands for "open source intelligence" and describes the obtaining of information from public, freely

accessible sources. There is no further connection to the version of the term which is used in the context of information processing.

HUMINT. This stands for "human intelligence", or the acquisition of information from human sources – what is traditionally most usually associated with intelligence service work.

SIGINT. This stands for "signals intelligence", which basically consists of telecommunications and electronic intelligence.

It is no coincidence that these terms either originate from or are attributable to the sphere of American intelligence services.

OSINT: open source intelligence

The acquisition of information through collecting and analysing public documents forms the basis of every kind of spying. This includes, for example, freely available information from newspapers, magazines and other media, company databases or registers of associations and also trade fairs at which the target company has a stand. A visit to the exhibition booth as an interested party – without revealing one's identity – may possibly reveal decisive added value as to current and future activities. OSINT may even include quite simple activities such as observing the works trucks at certain company locations, which permits conclusions about turnover and market development.

In addition, trade congresses at which employees of the target company play an active role, for example as presenters or participants in a podium discussion, are particularly rewarding. They often already disclose more information in their presentation than is in the interests of the company; questions from the public are mostly also just as willingly answered. Skilled experts in particular are rarely adequately trained for public relations work and tend to communicate more confidential details in a conversation between supposed peers than is advisable from the company's point of view. A professional dialogue with these experts is also possible outside of the world of conferences and congresses if a suitable pretext can be found. A suitable cover story is, of course, a prerequisite for a successful approach – and once again points beyond OSINT towards HUMINT as already discussed.

Similar research successes are possible in the case of research-driven companies if experts are identified and their publications in specialist media analysed. This applies not only to the employees themselves but also to possible partner organisations from the field of research and their specialist staff.

Another very simple and also totally legal approach is intensive Internet research of the target company and its key staff. Not infrequently, companies reveal more about themselves in this way than necessary. Documents which are only intended for internal use are quite frequently published on the Internet by accident. They may well only be online for a few hours until someone notices the error, but a well-conceived observation strategy can very quickly take advantage of just such an error.

Of course, it is also possible to wait for opportunities during which more information is accessible than usual. This is regularly the case during negotiations on joint ventures or takeovers. It is not inconceivable for an enquiry to be initiated with the aim of inducing just such a situation. However, the extent to which information gained in this way can be designated as freely accessible is definitely a matter of definition.

Covert requests for quotations are frequently used to obtain price information or detailed technical product information. This approach, which is also known as mystery shopping, entails everything from mere enquiries to comprehensive calls for tenders being made purposefully and without any intention of buying. Here, too, a suitable cover story is decisive for success or, in other words, to receive valid detailed information. Possible starting points are specialised market research agencies which sometimes prepare, perform and analyse such enquiries in collaboration with companies which may be considered as potential customers for the company to be spied on.

Up to this point, the arsenal of approaches still sounds acceptable. Almost nobody would object to solely using freely available information to get an idea of the competition and of their own market environment. Thus it is not surprising that the methods briefly described here belong to the tools of a discipline which distances itself explicitly from intelligence service and espionage work, known as competitive intelligence (CI) – also originating from the United States.

HUMINT: human intelligence

HUMINT involves the acquisition of information from human sources. Apart from the intelligence service world, HUMINT also describes a major part of the work of journalists, qualitative market researchers and police and justice authorities. Its decisive characteristic is that people are always approached; they frequently make themselves available voluntarily and sometimes even at no cost.

The ways of acquiring information are varied. One possibility is the exploitation of conversation situations at trade exhibitions and congresses, which strictly speaking falls under OSINT as already stated. However, under certain circumstances, advanced questioning techniques help to coax out of conversation partners – or rather victims – things which they didn't really want to reveal. The boundaries between OSINT and HUMINT, which is also known as social manipulation or more often as social engineering, are fluid. Through fraudulent misrepresentation, the victim's living environment is spied on with the aim of using it to get at confidential information at a later date. This may not be the ultimate aim of the espionage activities but, like access passwords, serves to get at the actual information wanted. The target person has no idea that he or she is being misused for the purposes of third parties either during the skimming of information during conversations or during social engineering.

That is, of course, not the only situation in which HUMINT is involved. It is just as important to build on the disloyalty of individual employees, either through financial benefits or the simple exploitation of the feelings of an employee who is possibly frustrated by their working environment. Attempts at blackmail in which an employee is spied on or purposefully manoeuvred into compromising situations and then forced to cooperate through corresponding pressure should also be seen in this context.

I used the general term "employee" rather than "key personnel" deliberately in the last paragraph because often it is enough to approach a trainee, a cleaner or some other person and force them to cooperate. They often have uncontrolled access to offices and documents and can also copy important information and pass it on even without precise specialist knowledge.

Company employees are not always actively involved. Long-term espionage activities can, for example, also be contemplated by smuggling in suitable staff. Job adverts are purposefully combed through and suitable applicants passed on to companies; references and application documents are manipulated accordingly. Such activities are, however, fairly rare, since they require long-term planning to achieve tangible results.

SIGINT: signals intelligence

SIGINT stands for the acquisition of information by means of electronic measures. This includes well-known classics such as bugging offices and conference or hotel rooms. It also includes the interception of radio transmissions in all conceivable forms. This is not just a matter of speech transmission but also the use of monitoring devices such as cordless keyboards. Bugging telecommunications generally falls under SIGINT. This includes not only bugging at service-provider level but also in some cases tapping into company phone lines. Observation or visual monitoring, for example by means of concealed cameras on company premises, should not be forgotten when contemplating SIGINT.

With the increasing networking of our living and working world, the areas of use for SIGINT are increasingly extending up to completely new application areas. It now also includes the production and evaluation of movement profiles for SIGINT based on the espionage target's mobile phone use.

COMINT, ELINT and TECHINT

The term COMINT for communications intelligence is also used in connection with espionage activities as a subcategory of SIGINT. The second complementary designation is ELINT (electronic intelligence), which involves recording and analysing electronic signals. The term TECHINT (technical intelligence) is also occasionally used. This embraces the use of technical aids to collect information – which cannot be clearly differentiated from SIGINT.

To a certain degree, these aforementioned terms are obsolete in relation to modern infrastructures with which it is no longer possible to clearly differentiate between information technology (IT) and telecommunications (TC). Consider, for example, a modern phone switchboard system as a target for an espionage attack: nowadays, such a system mainly consists of one piece of software which runs on a more or less standard server. Is a switchboard system in such a modern design IT or TC? Even experts wrestle in vain for clear answers. A separation between IT and TC makes little sense given the current state of technical development; accordingly, this is not differentiated unnecessarily in the following sections.

At the limits of law and ethics

The intelligence service abbreviations OSINT, HUMINT and SIGINT in neutral, official language reveal very little of the legal and ethical limits which are exceeded in the course of espionage activities. At a superficial glance, it is often forgotten that a part of these instruments can be used completely legally and partly also without ethical problems. For this reason, the term "competitive intelligence" is illuminated next and depicted with regard to its relation to the "dark side" of information acquisition – espionage to the detriment of companies.

Competitive intelligence

The relatively new discipline of competitive or competitor intelligence involves finding out as much as possible about your own company's competitors and their plans without straying into illegality. Competitive intelligence (CI) designates the systematic and permanent collection and analysis and also (internal) distribution of information on competitors and their products and services. This also includes market developments, sector trends, patent applications, new technologies and under certain circumstances even customer expectations, although there is not necessarily a clear differentiation from classical market research. Put another way and without bias, CI is knowledge of the competition's plans and the use of this knowledge to increase a company's own competitiveness – and also to reduce the risk of bad business decisions.

In its simplest form, a CI project consists of three elements: first, it is important to define what information should be collected. Normally, things begin with secondary research. This is what is defined previously under OSINT: all potentially relevant information is collected from publicly accessible sources, including company reports, registry entries, patent applications, court decisions, media reports, job adverts, blog entries and web content. This list can become much longer depending on the target and the content of the assignment.

This is typically followed by a phase of primary research – in other words, talking to people. In practise, secondary research mainly serves to identify the "right" people who are suitable for a conversation. The content provided by secondary research serves as a starting point for the topic and makes the CI researcher a well-informed conversation partner whom the target believes is worth talking to – mostly under false pretences and with false expectations as regards ethical considerations. The main difference to industrial espionage is the limitation to legally available information, although there is a substantial grey area which is often encroached upon in practise.

The process of competitive intelligence follows the so-called intelligence cycle. This is an information acquisition and analysis concept which was first described by intelligence services in the 1960s. This process consists mainly of the following steps (Deltl 2008):

- Planning. Formulation of information requirements, definition of key intelligence topics (KITs) and, derived from these, key intelligence questions (KIQs);
- Acquiring data and collecting information (based on KITs and KIQs). Primary sources are sector experts, (former) employees of competitors, customers, suppliers, dealers, trade exhibitions and congresses. Secondary sources are company reports, chambers of trade, lenders, market research and company information services, sector magazines, newspapers, the Internet, patents or specialist databases;
- Sorting of finds, filtering and editing. Translations of foreign-language sources, evaluation, structuring, interpretation and electronic storage of the information acquired.
- Analysing findings and editing results. Benchmarking; strengths, weaknesses, opportunities and threats (SWOT) analysis; competitor profiling; sector structure analysis; simulation models and war gaming;
- Making recommendations. Development and deduction of recommendations for decision making;
- Distributing results. Compilation of a CI report from draft to approval and handover to decision makers.

In continental Europe, CI has only been known as a discipline since the 1990s and is only taught at a few universities. It's different in North America and the United Kingdom: the beginning of the idea behind CI can be found in the United States in the 1970s, although CI was initially exclusively part of market research. A study by the economics professor Michael E. Porter, who teaches at Harvard University, was decisive for the breakthrough of this idea and its broad acceptance in both companies and educational facilities. His publication titled *Competitive Strategy* (Porter 1980) is regarded as the trailblazer for the entire debate about the collection and analysis of information on competitors.

CI was picked up and widely promoted by the Society of Competitive Professionals (SCIP, since renamed Strategic and Competitive Professionals with the same acronym), which was founded in 1986. This developed not only a wide common definition of CI but also a kind of body of knowledge and above all a code of ethics. However, even on closer examination it is difficult to decide whether certain behaviour in a competitive context is ethically proper or unacceptable and depends on the cultural or temporal context: a course of action which appears totally harmless here today can perhaps cause big problems tomorrow in another country.

In 2001, thee American management consultancy Fuld provided an interesting study on the question of cultural differences in evaluating whether certain CI practises are ethically proper (Fuld 2001). This study introduced various scenarios and presented them to study participants from North America and Europe for them to evaluate. More than 100 CI professionals from North America and Europe – in other words, people who deal intensively with the topic in their professional lives – were interviewed. Participants in the investigation were first confronted with different scenarios and then asked to evaluate them as "normal behaviour", "aggressive behaviour" (but still acceptable), "unethical behaviour" or "illegal behaviour".

- Documents in a conference hotel (scenario 1). It comes to your knowledge that your competitor is holding a management conference in a certain hotel. You drop by towards the end of the conference to see whether anyone has left behind any (internal) documents.

    - Results: Less than 10 percent of those questioned saw this as normal CI procedure. Some 10 percent of Europeans were of the opinion that this would be illegal, whilst only a few Americans were of the same opinion. Around 50 percent of all nations questioned characterised the situation as aggressive, and 42 percent of Americans and a third of Europeans questioned regarded this behaviour to be unethical.

- Conversation in a plane (scenario 2). You are sitting in a plane and happen to hear an employee of a competitor speaking to his neighbour and passing on information which appears to be confidential. Neither of them knows who you are and that you can hear the conversation.

    - Results: 70 to 80 percent of respondents see this as normal activity. Only 20 percent regarded this as aggressive, a small group of American managers as unethical and nobody as illegal.

- At a trade exhibition without a name badge (scenario 3). You visit a trade exhibition. You remove the name plate which identifies you as a competitor and then go to a stand and indicate that you are interested in the product being presented.

    - Results: Unlike with the two previous scenarios, American and European participants evaluate this scenario differently; 56 percent of Europeans regarded this approach as normal but only around 10 percent of Americans were of the same opinion. Around a third of those questioned from both regions evaluated this behaviour as aggressive. Half of the Americans and some 11 percent of Europeans considered this behaviour to be unethical and a small number of Americans even thought it illegal.

- Without a name badge in an exhibitor's private area at a trade fair (scenario 4). You visit a trade fair. You remove the name plate which identifies you as a competitor and then go to a stand and enter a private area which is designated as being for customers of company X.

- Results: Almost half of all Americans saw this as unethical, and 44 percent even said it was illegal. Less than 10 percent of Americans considered it normal or aggressive. In comparison, 39 percent of Europeans regarded this behaviour as aggressive and 55 percent as unethical.

The conclusion of the study was that most of those questioned had internalised the principles required by CI but interpreted them differently. There were significant differences between North Americans and Europeans – in other words, between two cultures which are really regarded as being similar. Although Fuld did not raise the question, it virtually raises itself: how can we assume that other cultures – think of China – share our fundamental concepts and values when dealing with information from third parties if there are already such significant differences between North America and Europe?

A generally acceptable classification can definitely be obtained by using the ethics guidelines of the SCIP organisation as orientation. A traffic-light code is introduced in the book titled *Competitive Intelligence in Practise* (Pfaff 2005): green stands for legal and fair play, yellow for the border areas where it is ethically questionable and red for illegal – what the author regards as industrial espionage. Amongst others, the following examples are given:

green: evaluating trade exhibitions, information brochures, publications, advertising materials, information on the Internet, press releases, conferences and congresses, information obtained from field sales and so forth;
yellow: evaluating documents accidentally left lying around, browsing through appointment schedules, pretend negotiations (mystery shopping) and so forth;
red: cracking passwords, bugging rooms, tapping phones, sounding out competitors' employees, smuggling in moles, theft, bribery and so forth.

This list provides a helpful delimitation to the broad field of industrial espionage, the core of the observations in this book. As already mentioned, we may not, however, assume that similar perceptions to the ones we are familiar with exist in other cultures. To argue here is risky: it is very easy to be confronted with accusations if you point out the cultural differences between the Western world and China and the constantly evoked "imitation as veneration of the master" for China as the alleged mainspring for developments there. It is even more dangerous to compare the socialism that was impressed on Eastern Europe for many years with reality in Western Europe: in a joint research project by Duke University and the Ludwig-Maximilians University in Munich (Ariely 2014), it was established in an abstract behavioural science experiment that people who lived under socialism for many years tend to cheat more often than others. This result is above all interesting in relation to Eastern European states and the espionage activities which emanate from there at the expense of European and North American companies, because although we all see ourselves as part of the Western civilization, that doesn't mean we automatically share the same values in detail.

Espionage at the expense of companies

For espionage targeted at companies, ethical and legal limits no longer play a role. It is purely a matter of getting the desired results and leaving as few traces as possible.

The ways of getting at the desired information are manifold. Anyone who watches spy movies is familiar with the scene in which the hero enters the boss's office over the roof, past cameras and alarm systems, cracks the safe with the secret plans and manages to get out of the building just a few seconds before security comes round the corner. This has little to do with reality. However, there are cases where a building or a temporarily used living space such as a hotel room or a vehicle are broken into to steal information or to obtain company secrets by means of a bug planted there. However, the indirect way is chosen much more often – positioning an employee in the company or recruiting someone who works there or an external person who has corresponding access, for example a cleaner.

The methods are as varied as the attackers and their targets. Companies are monitored by bugs being placed or suitable equipment used from outside. Directional microphones are used just as often as devices which receive emissions from cordless keyboards and monitors and can display the information in plain text. The new thing in the networked age is cyberespionage, technical attacks via the Internet connection. For this, the attacker does not even need to be anywhere near the target object: an Internet connection somewhere in the world is enough to attack practically any company. To what extent these and other methods indicated lead to success is, however, a different question.

Espionage as a business model

Industrial espionage is not always an activity which a company needs to take into their own hands. All around the world there are lots of service providers which are happy to act under cover of a legal company name when it comes to covering a specific information requirement. This mostly happens in secret, although sometimes totally publicly. A business partner of mine noticed a stand at an exhibition in Moscow where former secret service agents advertised their kind of information acquisition quite openly – in several languages and with a "guarantee of success". However, the corresponding website lost itself in vagueness about the effectiveness of market researchers who were engaged as employees.

The existence of such research companies was also known of in the United States and in Great Britain. More than a few of these companies, who sometimes act as private detectives, employ former intelligence service staff or policemen. It can be assumed that the odd enquiry is still dealt with via ex-colleagues who are still in the service of the state. Such companies also occasionally use tools which are normally only available to state bodies. It is an extremely opaque but fascinating sector which has developed here.

At the 2017 Mobile World Congress in Barcelona, Spain, there were several vendors who sell IT and telecommunication "forensic" tools and services. Other software programmes and devices which can be used to spy on your competitor are marketed as child or employee surveillance tools and even instruct the buyer that he or she needs to get consent of the target before implementing this solution, in the same way your car navigation system reminds you that you are responsible for driving and therefore should not allow yourself to be distracted by it.

Anyone can be affected

Company leaders, IT bosses or security representatives typically do not exhibit signs of nervousness and insecurity when discussing their assessment of the possible theft of company secrets. Just a few years ago the attitude that dominated was "we won't be affected, we're too small or too unimportant or too unknown".

This attitude has now fundamentally changed as a result of constant security incidents which have been reported in the media. However, hardly any of those interviewed have a clear strategy for dealing with these threats to company security. In addition, the true picture of their risk situation is distorted in many cases by the marketing efforts of many IT security companies, which promote their respective product as the most important part of a functioning defence strategy against the hazards of cyberespionage and cybercrime.

The examples discussed in Chapters 3 and 4 very clearly show that literally anyone can be affected. Whether the organization is a global corporation or a one-man show is irrelevant if the competition has a strong interest in internal company matters. The author Steven Fink even argues in his book *Sticky Fingers: Managing the Global Risk of Economic Espionage* (2002) that since smaller businesses typically have more competitors than large corporations, they can even be more exposed to corporate espionage. It is also not possible to exclude individual sectors from a risk assessment, although there are of course sectors which are particularly worthwhile targets due to their know-how: these include companies in the fields of armaments, microelectronics, chemicals, pharmaceuticals and genetic engineering.

This attitude is also confirmed by experts in the field: "The size of a company is not in the least decisive but rather whether a company has innovative specialist knowledge. That can be a company with ten employees or a large concern" (Proschko 2012). The target is usually "development data and innovations in high technology but equally the know-how of medium-sized companies and strategic information on company plans" (OVB 2013). Does this mean that building contractors or sawmill operators have less cause to worry?

A director of a well-known internationally operating construction company once phrased this for me as follows: "I work to the same plans with the same machinery, materials and tools and even the same subcontractors as my competitors. What does the competition not know that I do?" The answer is simple: the one big decisive difference is the price calculation. If the competition gets hold of it they can easily offer the best quote in tenders. There are indeed indications that information on pricing is one of the most frequent reasons for spying on the competition.

The notion that spies are only interested in secret formulae is therefore misleading. In the right combination, apparent trivialities can allow the attacker to make detailed conclusions. It is, for example, enough to know that several directors of Interbrew breweries have just arrived at the provincial airport of Paderborn-Lippstadt to draw conclusions about a possible takeover in the industry as long as one is aware of the background: Paderborn-Lippstadt is the closest airport to the Sauerland region with its many large breweries. Context is important! Such information, which initially appears banal, can supply important munition for working out counterstrategies or disruptive action. In competitive markets there is no such thing as a trivial information.

The following can be interesting targets for espionage directed at companies – with no guarantee of completeness: the current and future location of members of senior management and specialists, supervisory board and management protocols, tenders, identity documents and access control information, construction and land-use plans, design templates, purchase prices, inventions, fault and quality reports, manufacturing details, employee salaries and bonuses, profit and turnover calculations, innovative ideas from workshops or internal company competitions, calculations, purchase intentions of all kinds, layout plans, warehouse stocks, supplier lists, supplier and service contracts, logistics information, material samples, trade exhibition strategies, passwords and access data, patent applications, employees' personal data (especially that of management), pilot projects and experiments, start-up investments, product components, travel plans and congress visits, road maps for product variants or marketing activities, security systems, strategy concepts, study results, detailed technical knowledge, direct phone numbers, test arrangements and results, transport routes and times, accident analyses and reports, company key data, intentions to sell, contract details, sales strategies, merchandise samples, payment and account data and access facilities via Internet or VPN. Much of this information is anything but confidential, but if collected, analysed and concentrated, it may possibly form the basis for an attack on central company data.

Hard facts and reliable statistics on the latest targets of competitor espionage are, however, rare. A study on the topic of economically motivated espionage activities produced on behalf of American government authorities by Richard Heffernan, the director of a company which evaluates business risks and a member of the advisory board of the National Counterintelligence Center (NACIC), showed that the most important espionage targets are distributed as follows: 56 percent on price information, 33 percent on product development information, 6 percent on manufacturing technology information and the remaining 5 percent on other attack targets. Whether this information is still valid and up to date under current conditions and whether it can be transferred to your home country is doubtful.

In 2013, the auditing company Ernst & Young came to a rather more differentiated result in their study titled *Data Theft*, for which 400 companies were interviewed. According to this, the main espionage targets by business area are 52 percent research and development; 21 percent sales; 14 percent production; 11 percent finance, accounting and credit department; and 11 percent staff. From my work with companies in Western Europe, I know of many cases in which just price information was to be targeted but which ultimately touched on various business areas.

Of course, not every company is equally at risk. So-called company-specific risks depend on the competitive situation in the sector as well as the company's own position in the domestic or global market. In summary, it can be said that global players are always at risk, although as some of the following examples show, espionage attacks do not always originate from direct competitors. Sometimes, buyers and partner companies are out to extend their own business potential. Caution is therefore advised in all directions.

3 From old-school espionage to modern methods of attack

When we speak of economically motivated espionage today, most people have certain perceptions or rather clichés in their minds, from a bug under the conference table in the meeting room, to the spy who has somehow sneaked in and photographed secret documents with a miniature camera. Our conceptual world is just as much characterised by cultural prejudices: industrial spies, for example, have to be from China. The "yellow peril" frequently invoked in the press is a plausible picture of perceived espionage risks. Since the end of the Cold War, the "bad Russian" has also had to serve as a symbol for the dangers which threaten our companies and our economy through espionage. The situation was not always so clear: looking back into the past, the Western world didn't always come off that well.

Eavesdropping on the opposition has traditionally been a widespread practise since ancient times. In the 4th century BC, the Tyrant of Syracuse supposedly kept Attic prisoners of war in an artificially created cave known as the Ear of Dionysius with special acoustics in order to eavesdrop on what his enemies were planning. The book titled *Journey to the Orient* by Friedrich Wilhelm Hackländer describes the structure of this facility as follows (Hackländer 1846):

> The cave itself is around eighty paces long, meandering in shape and leads to a small funnel-shaped, tapering chamber in which Dionysius had the prisoners chained to the walls with iron rings. Together with the sides, the ceiling forms an almost Gothic arch, and at the top a foot deep round channel has been hewn out which runs above through the passageway, breaks through the right wall just a few feet before the entrance and leads into the small chamber which is visible from outside. The latter is the so-called Ear of Dionysius in which the tyrant would eavesdrop on the talk of the prisoners incarcerated in the chamber at the end of the cave.

Whether this use, which is mentioned in this and other reports, was intended, remains unclear, but local travel guides are happy to tell the story to anyone who comes past even today.

The fascination of eavesdropping gripped not only the well-known 19th-century author Hackländer but also the polymath Athanasius Kicher almost 200 years before. In his book *Musurgia Universalis*, published in 1662, which he devoted to music, he described various architectural models for acoustic surveillance. The ingredients are always very similar: the sound is collected in a large funnel and directed through a passageway in the shape of a snail's shell. Whether his remarks had any further practical basis or came purely from the fascination for the new from which his multifaceted work emanated is not clear.

No evidence has survived of an actual case in which such structural bugging facilities played any role in an economic conflict. But we can safely assume that there were definitely eavesdroppers at the courts of the big reigning royal families with a view for acquiring economic advantages. The history of art alone is full of motifs in which somebody is eavesdropping, usually behind a door – completely without technical equipment.

The dawn of economic espionage

The cases from the beginnings of economic espionage handed down and documented here are all characterised by the fact that the spying was narrowly targeted. Certain technical processes or knowledge were always the main point of interest. Spies sometimes had to contend with years of research and not infrequently even risk their lives in order to fathom them. The following examples not only show how it all began but also provide proof of the changes in the problems faced and the methods of attack over the course of time.

The magic of silk

Silk originated from China. For a long time, how silk was manufactured remained a closely guarded secret and was the basis for lucrative trade between East and West. It gave the Silk Road, the trade route between China and Europe, its name. At times, silk was even counterbalanced with gold.

Many myths surround how the manufacture of silk found its way out of China despite strict security measures – the export of silkworms or their eggs was punishable by death. It is alleged that at the beginning of the 5th century AD, the daughter of the Chinese emperor smuggled silkworm eggs and mulberry tree seeds to Kothan in today's Myanmar in her headdress because she didn't want to do without her silk dresses after her marriage to the count. From Kothan, knowledge of silk manufacture spread to Japan and India (Silk 2008). In another version of the story, the king of Kothan and the husband of precisely this lady of Chinese origin was the driving force and persuaded her to do some smuggling. This could be regarded as the first more or less precisely documented case of economically motivated espionage at a global level.

Also in the 6th century, from the year 522, there are reports that two monks succeeded in smuggling both silkworm eggs and mulberry tree seeds to Byzantium in cavities in their hiking poles. The manufacture of silk began in the Mediterranean area on the basis of these souvenirs. With this, the Chinese monopoly on silk production was definitively history even if the quality of the end product could not compete with the Chinese original for a long time. In other words, it would have been a good idea to gather more precise information about production processes, as a rudimentary knowledge of silk spinning was not enough to keep up with the production techniques in China, which had been refined over a period of thousands of years.

At any rate, this early case of spying on the competition shows not only a considerable investment of time but also immense personal risks. From a contemporary point of view, it was hardly worth it for Europe in the case of silk: the most important production centres today are Brazil, China, Thailand, India and Japan.

The power of fire

With few exceptions, until modern times it was military secrets which were much sought after but closely guarded. But confidentiality only seldom succeeded for any length of time: technical innovations in weapons and improvements in existing systems were quickly copied by friend and foe alike. Only one single case is known of where it was possible to keep a genuine "miracle weapon" – a weapon which was decisive for the outcome of war – secret for centuries.

This was Greek fire, the chemical composition and design of which is still controversial even today. It was a naval weapon with which enemy ships could be set alight. In the 7th century, this Greek fire helped to repel an attack on the Arab fleet at Byzantium for the first time. Historians connect this weapon with the long-lived success of the empire through to the 15th century. Or in other words, economic prosperity was decisively influenced by keeping this military secret safe. On the other hand, examples showing the successful spying out of military secrets are legion up to the present day.

The broken mirror

It was only much later that processes and technologies which promised economic benefits became the main focus of spying activities. At the same time, important secrets were protected by a variety of means: on Murano, an island in the Venetian Lagoon, the glassmakers were forbidden from leaving the island on pain of severe punishment – treason was punishable by death – obviously an effective approach, since it took centuries before the Venetian technologies were explored or reverse engineered.

Nowadays, a mirror is nothing special for anyone. That was completely different in the Middle Ages. Only a few extremely rich people compared to today's standards could afford a mirror. Around 1300, Venetian glassblowers on Murano succeeded in making mirrors out of glass for the very first time. This technical head start for the Venetian glass- and mirror makers concentrated on Murano was of interest to spies from all over the rest of Europe. But it was agents of Louis XIV, the Sun King, who first succeeded in bringing knowledge of how to make mirrors to France – his wish for a grand hall of mirrors in the Chateau of

Versailles would otherwise hardly have been realisable at Venetian prices. It was possible to entice a number of master craftsmen in glassmaking from Murano to France with powers of persuasion and financial promises. There, production was not only continued but also perfected further. And as a result of French espionage activities, the art of glassmaking spread across all of Europe.

The example of Murano clearly shows that it can definitely be worth protecting business secrets from third parties. The role of the state is also interesting, which here held its protective hand over Murano in the form of the Council of Venice as an important source for the wealth of the lagoon city.

On the way to paper

Ulman Stromer was one of the Nuremberg merchant Heinrich Stromer's 18 children. He was born into a sizeable family business with subsidiaries in Barcelona, Genoa, Milan and Krakow. His name is associated with the first paper mill north of the Alps in a small town called Pegnitz, which started operation in 1390. One detail in Stromer's biography which is usually forgotten is the question as to how he as a Nuremburg spice merchant acquired knowledge of how to manufacture paper in the first place.

In 1389, Stromer "imported" the formula for producing paper from Andalusia, which was Arabic in those days. The first European paper production had been established in Xàtiva in 1150. The duration of Stromer's success was, however, limited: he died of the plague in 1407 and the trading house went bankrupt in 1434, but a descendant was able to rescue the paper mill before it burnt down (NUE 2017).

Stromer's role in the spread of paper clearly shows that the successful spying out of know-how can change the course of the world. For book printing as developed by Johannes Gutenberg in 1445 in Mainz would not have been conceivable without sufficient paper available at an economic price. The question is how our cultural history would have run without this early access to cheap paper resources.

Russian economic development

The Russian czar Peter the Great was a ruler who liked to take matters into his own hands. His declared goal in life was to reform the then backwards Russian state based on the European model. From 1697 to 1698 he organised a so-called Great Legation to various European countries. He himself travelled incognito under the name of Piotr Michailov as a non-commissioned officer of the Preobrazhensky Regiment.

During this time, the czar worked as a craftsman in shipbuilding in Zaandam and Amsterdam. He especially wanted to learn in relation to his own fleet. He also recruited numerous specialists – not only for shipbuilding but also for his dream of a new world-class Russian state and a new capital at St. Petersburg.

From a historical point of view, it remained an absolute exception for a leader, above all a head of state, to operate undercover personally. The czar's will to succeed must have been particularly strong.

How porcelain came to Europe

The history of porcelain in Europe is closely associated with Père d'Entrecolles. From all that we know about him today, this French Jesuit monk was in China at the beginning of the 18th century – some sources claim he was active as an industrial spy. At this time, China was foremost in the manufacture of high-quality porcelain, a product which had long established itself as a valuable trading commodity in European ruling houses.

Père d'Entrecolles used his time in China to learn about porcelain manufacture: he visited production facilities, studied Chinese books and received much detailed information from locals, particularly from people who worked in the porcelain sector. He noted the knowledge he gathered between 1712 and 1772 in letters which he sent to France. Later, he invoked curiosity as the reason for his research but also wrote that the precise description of the details of this work could be useful in Europe. How right he was! He helped start the porcelain business in Europe with his findings, although he was not the only one showing a deep interest in production of what once called white gold.

In 1717, a German, Johann Friedrich Böttger, started to fire up the popular white porcelain in kilns in a factory on the Albrechtsburg in Meissen. He found a near-perfect mixture of elements for producing white porcelain by visiting other manufacturers and studying their production technology. The rest of the development is the stuff of legend: porcelain factories with resounding names such as Meissener or Nymphenburger and ultimately a whole sector right across Europe resulted from this early case of economically motivated espionage.

The secret of tea

What occurs to you when you hear the word "tea"? Perhaps the English tradition of five o'clock tea, and most probably India and Ceylon as the main countries where tea is grown. But the history of tea in the Western world has an astounding secret in store.

In the 19th century, Great Britain was dependent on deliveries from China, because at that time it held the monopoly on tea. The London East India Company hired a Scottish botanist and adventurer with the wonderful name of Robert Fortune to discover China's tea secret. Disguised as a Chinese merchant, he not only advanced into areas which were forbidden for foreigners but also succeeded in bringing back plants and seeds as well as know-how about the successful cultivation and processing of the plants. He brought this knowledge to India, then ruled by the English (TEA 2010), where tea production proceeded to overtake that of China during his lifetime. For Sarah Rose, author of the book titled *For All the Tea in China*, which deals knowledgeably with the story surrounding Robert Fortune, this is the "largest single incidence of spying on the competition in the history of the world" (Bloomberg 2011).

It is remarkable that, as with all cases of espionage from the preindustrial and early industrial ages, considerable personal effort was required to achieve the desired goal. And for precisely this reason, Fortune remained in China for a number of years and took a great risk, as other economic spies have before and since.

The beginning of the English textile industry

In many ways, the start of industrialisation was characterised by espionage activities. Innovations in production processes were a popular target for resourceful entrepreneurs in many different countries. The British textile industry was thus founded to a large extent on the activities of John Lombe, who travelled to Piedmont in 1714 to spy out an important production secret of the then-leading silk-weaving mill in Lucca. In his book *Roads to Xanadu: East and West in the Making of the Modern World*, John Merson described in detail the particularly complex procedure in this case (Merson 1989):

> Daringly, Lombe decided to become an industrial spy. He learned Italian, draughtsmanship and Mathematics. [. . .] Lombe was able to secure the help of a Jesuit priest, who, the story goes, procured him a job as a machine winder in one of the spinning works in Lucca in return for payment of an "oblazione", a bribe.

On the basis of this, the spy succeeded in producing plan drawings of the throwing machine and major individual parts and to smuggle them to his brother. He was discovered but succeeded in escaping abroad in dramatic circumstances. Immediately on his arrival in Great Britain, he submitted a patent for precisely the machines he had drawn even before he used this knowledge to set up the first water-powered textile factory in England. This is still regarded as the prototype of modern textile production today.

John Lombe himself came to a bleak end some years later: he died in 1722 at the age of 29, six years after his return from Italy. An Italian woman who Lombe had employed after setting up his factory and who vanished after his demise was allegedly involved in his death. Many contemporary witnesses at the time were of the opinion that Lombe was the victim of a revenge poisoning attack. Beyond the end of the story, which would have made a good film, the case is absolutely prototypical for the beginnings of industrial espionage: a great deal of time and effort combined with considerable personal risk.

The end of the rubber monopoly

Around 1840, Charles Goodyear – a well-known tyre company still bears his name today – discovered vulcanisation, a process by which rubber can be made resistant to mechanical stress and also chemical and atmospheric influences. Natural rubber became vulcanised rubber. A huge demand grew up for this raw material. At that time, Brazil had a monopoly on rubber production.

In 1876, the Englishman Henry Wickham tried to attack this monopoly. He travelled to Brazil to collect rubber tree seeds. The ban on exporting seeds, seedlings or whole rubber tree plants didn't put him off. According to reports of the time, Wickham disguised himself as an orchid collector and brought around 70,000 seeds out of the country. From them, around 2,000 seedlings were grown in the greenhouses of the Royal Botanical Gardens and then transported to Malaysia to put an end to the Brazilian monopoly by growing them there. Only eight seedlings survived the journey, but they were enough to successfully produce natural rubber in South East Asia.

Within 20 years after the start, almost 90 percent of the world's rubber requirement came from this region – the Brazilian monopoly ceased to exist. Prices also dropped together with the new source of supply. It can therefore definitely be said that this case of economically motivated espionage produced added value for the benefit of consumers worldwide. The English queen was of the same opinion and knighted Henry Wickham for his services to the kingdom.

By the way, Goodyear himself, who started the boom rolling, had to put up with extensive copying of his invention of vulcanisation, regardless of his patent.

The German steam engine

Carl Friedrich Bückling was a miner, inventor and industrial spy. At the instigation of Frederick II, king of Prussia (also known in history as Frederick the Great), he travelled to England to find out about the design of Watt-style steam engines. James Watt had patented his steam engine in 1769, and it became the leading light of the industrial revolution.

The specific reason for Bückling's journey was copper slate mining in Hettstedt in Saxony-Anhalt. There, work on the development of a new shaft had reached the limits of conventional technology: the pumps which were then normally operated by horses could not provide enough power to permanently pump off the water flowing into the shaft. A quotation for a machine from Boulton and Watt had been obtained beforehand, but it had not been possible to reach an agreement.

Instead, Bückling was sent on a journey. He travelled to England twice until he had collected enough detailed information to be able build a copy of the machine. The first German steam engine went into operation on 23 August 1785. It took another two years of operation before everything worked reliably. Nevertheless, this engine was still in operation until 1848.

As hard as Krupp steel – thanks to some help from the English

The following version of the story of Krupp, nowadays ThyssenKrupp, can be found online on the company website (Krupp n.d.):

> On November 20, 1811, Friedrich Krupp establishes a factory with two partners for the making of English cast steel and all products therefrom. After he succeeds in making high-quality cast steel (crucible steel) in 1816, he begins production of tanner's tools, coining dies and unfinished rolls. In 1817 the Imperial Mint in Düsseldorf confirms the quality of Krupp cast steel. In 1818 Krupp supplies his first coining die to the Prussian mint head office in Berlin.

However, other sources present the story of the company rather less glamorously.

The main problem with steel production at that time was the carbon content. The English had succeeded in considerably improving the quality of steel by adding certain materials during the smelting process. The English defended their technological head start by prohibiting steelworkers from leaving England. All over Europe, numerous experiments attempted to identify the company secret behind English steel production. But nobody managed really satisfactory results, including initially Krupp – despite innumerable expensive attempts. "Up to autumn 1814, 30,000 Reichstalers flowed into the company which were complemented by earnings of just 1,422 Reichstalers", according to Harold James's book *Krupp: A History of the Legendary German Firm* (James 2012). In 1824, the company collapsed, although progress had meanwhile been made with the quality of steel, and Friedrich Krupp died in 1826.

It was not until 1839 that his son Alfred Krupp made a breakthrough after he was able to bring the formula back from a journey to England. He had had himself shown around steel production plants under the false name of Crip – at least that is what well-known Journalist Udo Ulfkotte claims in his controversial book *Industrial Espionage* (Ulfkotte 2001). Ulfkotte's further remarks are interesting: according to him, Alfred Krupp set up a works protective force, which was outstanding for the time, which was intended to prevent leaking of company secrets.

But Krupp was not alone in his thirst for knowledge: in 1823, the industrialist Eberhard Hoesch travelled to Sheffield together with the English engineer Samuel Dobbs, a specialist in steelworks construction, to study the latest technology in the British steel industry. Hoesch masqueraded as a factory machine merchant. As he began to show a bit too much interest in details, the ironworks foreman became suspicious and informed the police. He fled before he could be arrested and initially hid on the premises inside the chimney of a cooled-down furnace, but had to leave this in a hurry after workers fired it up. He escaped amongst the backstreets of Sheffield before he succeeded in returning to Germany via France. Despite the adventurous circumstances, Hoesch was successful and was subsequently able to duplicate production in his own steelworks.

The business secrets of the British steel industry were sought after not only in Germany. France sent engineers disguised as apprentices, and the Dutch and Americans also tried to find out details about the English steel industry. The Official Secrets Act was thereupon passed on 26 August 1889. This stated that (OSA 1889),

> where a person for the purpose of wrongfully obtaining information (i) enters or is in any part of a place belonging to Her Majesty the Queen, being a fortress, arsenal, factory, dockyard, camp, ship, office, or other like place, in which part he is not entitled to be; or (ii) when lawfully or unlawfully in any such place as aforesaid, either obtains any document, sketch, plan, model or knowledge of anything he is not entitled to obtain, or takes without lawful authority any sketch or plan, he shall be guilty of a misdemeanor, and on conviction be liable to imprisonment, with or without hard

labour, for a term not exceeding one year, or to a fine, or to both imprisonment and a fine.

With that, Great Britain had become the first country to pass a law against industrial espionage.

Espionage as an international business

Up to industrialisation, industrial espionage was mostly the work of ambitious individuals acting on their own who often put their own lives at risk to discover the knowledge of others. This changed after World War II. As the following examples show, it is now often large concerns which fight against each other in the battle for customers.

The dreaded copier

Espionage by means of a copier has a long tradition. During the Cold War, the United States used Xerox copiers to spy on the Soviet Union. In 1961, the CIA was looking for a means of accessing the Soviets' military secrets and found it via a photocopier in the Russian embassy in Washington, or rather in the servicing staff. A small camera was installed inside the technically highly complex Model 914 which photographed all documents photocopied by the machine at the same time. During the next maintenance visit, the Xerox service technician was able to collect the used film and replace it with a fresh one.

This procedure proved to be so successful that it was also used in other embassies. The whole thing was exposed by chance in 1969. But it wasn't the Soviets who discovered the espionage; rather it became known that an American company had used the same tactic against a competitor. This was the end of this kind of espionage – at least officially.

As we know since Edward Snowden's revelations and the Wikileaks "Vault7" publications, the NSA and the CIA use comparable procedures in which devices are provided with unwanted functionality, even though these are technically much more advanced. For example, Cisco routers are intercepted on the way to customer companies, the package is opened and the device is manipulated – an espionage technician on-site is no longer necessary.

Supersonic spies

The aeroplane of the future, nothing less than a revolution in air travel – that was to be Concorde. From Europe to New York in less than four hours was the promise of the supersonic passenger aeroplane, a child of the almost unclouded future optimism of the 1960s. Concorde was developed and built by a Franco-British joint effort. The maiden flight took place in 1969 and the plane went into commercial service in 1976.

A further supersonic plane came into being at almost the same time in the Soviet Union: the Tupolev TU-144, frequently mockingly called Concordski due to its similarity to Concorde. In fact, the TU-144 took its maiden flight before Concorde in 1969. It was the time of the Cold War; in addition to the fight for space, supersonic passenger planes were a further field in which technical superiority could be demonstrated, as the author Howard Moon wrote in his 1989 book *Soviet SST: The Techno-Politics of the Tupolev-144.*

An episode of the prizewinning American documentary series *Nova* broadcast on 27th January 1998 titled *Supersonic Spies* looked at the question of how this astounding similarity between the planes could have come about and also showed Howard Moon, who described the methods of the time as follows (Supersonic 1998):

> There were lists of different things for their people in the West to find. Exchange students, for example, helped pay their scholarship in the West by leafing through open source magazines. The information was brought back into Russia. There was a kind of a central collection agency that got all this material together, this army of about 10,000 grubs going through this very turgid, very, very sensitive, hard-to-understand technical material.

In addition, Soviet agents successfully infiltrated the Concorde production plant in France. The plans collected there were photographed on microfilm and brought back to the Soviet Union by couriers; other knowledge was transferred via coded radio transmissions. One of the Soviet agents was simultaneously aide-de-camp for the Aeroflot airline in Paris, which provided him with access to the aerospace sector. When he was finally discovered, he was carrying documents on Concorde's landing equipment. He was deported and later became vice-minister for civil aviation in the Soviet Union (Supersonic 1998). This example gives an indication of the variety of approaches in one and the same case and also how OSINT and genuine espionage activities work together for a common goal.

In 1978 and after, having carried a total of just 3,200 passengers, the TU-144 was taken out of service again and the project was ended for reasons of cost and complexity. Neither was Concorde blessed with lasting success: in 2003, it was taken out of service for economic reasons after a serious accident in 2000 in which 113 people died.

The fight for sovereignty in the air

To outsiders, the aerospace industry is a strange business: there only a few providers – for certain segments, just Airbus and Boeing – and customers are frequently state or state-controlled companies. At the same time, several million euros or dollars in turnover are at stake for every order negotiated.

In 1994, Airbus and Boeing were involved in negotiations with Saudi Arabian Airlines for an order with a volume of US$6 billion. The American Secret Service had intercepted faxes between the European Aeronautic Defence and

Space Company (EADS) subsidiary Airbus and the Saudi royal family and also tapped phone conversations and brought a bribery scandal to light – which wasn't one in the view of the Europeans. At the time of the negotiations, it was legal in Germany, France and other European countries to bribe important officials; the necessary expenses for this could even be offset against tax.

The deal still fell through for Airbus, and Boeing got the order. A classic case of industrial espionage? In the final analysis, it didn't matter to Airbus that the Americans allegedly wanted to take action against corruption: Airbus lost out (Airbus 2003).

When the secret service lends a hand

One of the best-known cases of espionage with an economic background is the so-called ICE case. In 1993, two providers were competing for an order worth billions for a high-speed train in South Korea. A consortium led by Siemens lost out to the Franco-British competitor GEC Alstom with their TGV. The competitor succeeded in undercutting all of Siemens's quotations and securing the order.

There were suspicions that Alstom had had support from the Direction Générale de la Sécurité (DGSE), the French secret service, in spying out the quotations from Germany. However, there was no ultimate proof or investigation.

Hopefully it's concrete

Rieder GmbH is an Austro-German manufacturer of fibre-reinforced concrete with its production facilities in Kolbermoor near Rosenheim in Bavaria. Components developed and produced by Rieder are used in the structural-facings sector, for example in the world championship stadium in Johannesburg.

A visitor from China came to Kolbermoor for a project meeting and a tour of the works as the representative of a possible partner company for a joint major order. During a tour of the works, a Rieder employee noticed that the guest was wearing a mini camera on his belt. An inspection of the camera data showed that the information documented about the product and production processes would have been enough to have the high-tech panels copied and counterfeited in China (OVB 2009).

The spy was given a suspended sentence by Munich district court in December 2009. "Since then, we deal with this issue more sensitively and screen potential partners more intensively", explained company spokeswoman Stephanie Jung (TAZ 2009). This example makes clear that, especially in the production environment, classical espionage techniques have not fallen into disuse. On this occasion it was purely thanks to an observant employee that any damage was prevented.

Gone with the wind

Aloys Wobben and his company Enercon have been developing wind turbines since 1984. With the boom in renewable energy, his company also grew after he had initially been ridiculed as a green crank. But success also brought competition – with an especially perfidious modus operandi against Enercon. *Manager Magazine* reported on the case in an article in 2008 (Manager Magazine 2008):

> His ingenuity fascinated managers of the US Kenetech Windpower company so much that they brazenly resorted to espionage – together with the NSA. [. . .] The NSA's scouts intercepted secret codes in Enercon's phone system and passed them on to Kenetech. The Kenetech spies used the data to get into an Enercon wind power plant and took time to anatomise it. The intruder copied the technology and had it patented in the USA. And then sued the Germans – allegedly for copying them.

The consequence for Enercon was an export ban lasting several years. However, Aloys Wobben survived this negative experience unscathed. According to a newspaper report in in the autumn of 2013, he was the richest citizen in Lower Saxony and was number 16 in the list of the richest Germans.

Sow the wind and reap the whirlwind

Enercon is not the only wind-power provider to suffer negative experiences and be spied on. But there is a completely different plot behind the next case: a company's largest customer became its enemy.

Sinovel is a Chinese manufacturer of wind turbines with worldwide sales and American Superconductor (AMSC) is one of Sinovel's suppliers. Amongst other things, AMSC produces software for connecting wind turbines to the electric network – a major component of any wind power plant. Until March 2011, Sinovel bought software and equipment from AMSC. At this time, AMSC had more than US$100 million in outstanding accounts from Sinovel alone. In addition, Sinovel had undertaken to buy further software and equipment for a further US$700 million from AMSC. But in that very month Sinovel suddenly stopped buying products from AMSC – to the total astonishment of its management. And in the same month, an Austrian employee of the Austrian subsidiary, Dejan Karabasevic, resigned from his post.

In June of the same year, an AMSC service technician discovered an unlicensed version of the operating software whilst servicing a Sinovel wind turbine in China. For fear of industrial espionage and licence theft, AMSC had in the past found a means of encrypting the software so that without the correct licence code it would only run for two weeks – as a kind of test installation. Both functions had been disabled in the software found by the technician. Internal investigations ultimately led to Dejan Karabasevic, who had exchanged a conspicuously high number of e-mails and Skype dialogues with Sinovel employees before giving notice. Further investigations made it clear that Karabasevic had come to an agreement with Sinovel – for a six-figure salary and a small apartment in Beijing. He was to download the software, make it available to the Chinese and modify and maintain it if necessary so that it worked with

Sinovel wind turbines. He was sentenced to a spell in prison in 2011 (Bayer 2013).

AMSC, on the other hand, is currently fighting for compensation from Sinovel before a Chinese court (Doom 2014). The company got into economic difficulties as a result of the attack by their former major customer: it had to lay off more than half of its staff and lost more than US$1 million in value on the stock market. According to other sources, however, Sinovel has meanwhile been forced to close several subsidiaries outside China due to the pressure being built up by AMSC (Cusick 2013). In any case, the wind-power sector is always good for an industrial espionage story.

Bad employees

The story of economically motivated espionage wouldn't be complete without a look at the role of the insider as the culprit. The breadth of cases involving insiders is enormous, whether they were smuggled in from outside or inveigled into theft due to professional frustration.

A French economic development programme

An interesting case of employee espionage happened in the United States at the beginning of the 1990s at Renaissance Software. This company was a start-up from Palo Alto in California which specialised in risk management software for banks with around 20 employees at the time. Marc Goldberg, a French national, handed in his notice in June 1990 because he wanted to return to his home country the following month. However, his behaviour changed noticeably in the remaining weeks before he left: whilst Goldberg, unlike other software developers, had never stayed at work until late in the evening before, he now did so regularly. His colleagues noticed this, and computers and copiers were prepared accordingly in order to document events.

They soon had something to show for this: on 8 July 1990, a Sunday, Marc Goldberg set to work, copied the source code of the software development implemented by Renaissance and duplicated other documents on the photocopier. The same day, the general manager and other employees hurried to the company, found their suspicions confirmed and then went looking for Goldberg in his apartment. He handed them the documents and a cassette from a computer tape drive – back then a normal medium for storing large quantities of data – which later turned out to be empty. The manager arranged an interview in his office for the next day but also immediately informed the police as he had seen a packed suitcase in the apartment. And so it was that soon after, Goldberg was arrested at San Francisco Airport as he attempted to board a flight to France.

Initially, everything pointed to it being a typical case of employee theft, but there was one spicy detail: the French consul in San Francisco and later also the French embassy in Washington tried to persuade Renaissance's management to drop their charges against Goldberg. Nevertheless, Goldberg was sentenced to one year in prison and three years' probation, a sentence which was subsequently commuted to 1,000 hours of community service work. Goldberg was permitted to leave for France in May 1991.

The strong involvement of French officials was quite astounding. However, Chantal Haage, press attaché at the consulate in San Francisco, denied that the French government had anything whatsoever to do with the case. It was, however, remarkable that Goldberg had travelled to the United States on a state-sponsored French promotion programme. And before he started work for Renaissance, he worked for Must Software in Norwalk, Connecticut, a subsidiary of the French state-owned Thomson-CSF concern. All just a coincidence, or a case of a state concern pulling the strings? At any rate, the intensive involvement of France in support of the accused left behind a lot of unanswered questions.

Betrayal by former employees

Eleven months suspended: that was the sentence for a former employee of the helicopter manufacturer Eurocopter for selling company documents to the Russian secret service. Eurocopter representatives hastened to announce that the company had not suffered any damage, as the documents were available to the authorities in Russia anyway due to the civil helicopter involved being registered there (AA 2008).

A typical case of financial necessity becoming the driving force behind spying activities. The mechanical engineer in financial difficulties received around €13,000 for his "work". It is, however, surprising that this kind of money was paid for documents which were publicly available anyway.

The Detroit and Wolfsburg Strangler

One of the darkest chapters in the history of the automotive industry is closely related to a manager called José Ignacio López. He was known by the not terribly flattering nickname of "the Strangler". López was the head of purchasing at General Motors (GM) and was known as a cost squeezer. In March 1993 he moved to Volkswagen (VW), also as head of purchasing, together with a team of workers.

GM accused López of having taken crates full of confidential material with him and took legal measures against VW. According to a report of *Spiegel* magazine in issue 33 (Spiegel 1993), several crates with GM material were indeed found in the apartment of a López employee. López denied these accusations but had to give up his post at Volkswagen in 1996 and then earn his living as a freelance consultant.

According to various media reports, the matter had come to light because the NSA had monitored internal VW video conferences and phone calls and passed on what they found to GM. GM then accused VW of industrial espionage and the illegal use of business secrets and took their competitor to court in the

United States. After a long legal battle, VW was to buy car parts from GM to the value of US$1 billion as a compensation.

Regardless of the question as to whether López-style cost squeezing actually represented a business secret of GM, one thing is remarkable about this case: the fixation on printed documents in boxes and folders. Storage media are not mentioned in any single accessible document on the events surrounding the Strangler. Today, almost 25 years later, it is in any case hardly imaginable that anyone would take crateloads of documents when they move from one company to another: a USB stick or a memory card should suffice as transport medium.

Bugs for everyone

In the summer of 2014, a spying scandal rocked the headquarters of the Ford motor company in Dearborn, Michigan, United States. Recording devices were found in several conference rooms. According to media reports, these were fitted under tables in conference rooms. The trail led to Sharon Leach, a graduate engineer, who worked in the hybrid systems sector.

If jumping to conclusions, one could take events as a further example of classic espionage activities and point out the long tradition of bugging. However, the recording technology discovered was by no means the kind of high-quality equipment available from spy shops. Quite the opposite: talk was of a "Sansa recording device" and an invoice from the online shop Buy.com, a brand of the Japanese trading company Rakuten, which is also present in Europe. Sansa is one of the last remaining manufacturers of MP3 players and offers a recording (dictation) function in some models. This capability is only limited by the size of the memory card and the battery life. But even with a simple model for around €40 it is possible to record everything which is said in a room for a whole day or longer. Eight such devices were found in this case.

Technical progress ensures that it is possible for anyone to spy extensively on a company with little effort. Unlike in the past, neither special technology nor specific sources of supply are required but simply a widely available device from an online shop or electrical superstore. Who can estimate how many similar cases there have already been and how many there constantly are?

Starwood versus Hilton

The hotel sector is also not immune to espionage activities. At first glance this may appear strange, for it is generally believed that it doesn't take much to get at a hotel's "company secrets": just book a room, check in and then keep your eyes open just as a hotel tester does, collect some detailed knowledge and draw conclusions.

Nevertheless, in April 2009 the Hilton hotel chain was sued by their competitor Starwood Hotels and Resorts for the theft of business secrets. Starwood stated that two former Starwood managers, who meanwhile worked for Hilton, had stolen business secrets from Starwood's W hotel brand and developed

Hilton's Denizen hotel concept on this basis. Specifically, the managers were accused of stealing confidential Starwood information from company computers. There was talk of a lorry load of documents which the two managers had allegedly downloaded. The diction had therefore changed little compared to the case between VW and GM already mentioned, although the documents in question were now in electronic form instead of in folders and therefore no longer had to be transported in packing cases.

The case was settled out of court in 2010: Hilton not only had to pay compensation but also could not bring any new luxury hotel brand on to the market until 2013 (Shapiro 2010). This example shows that it's not always about Paris Hilton when the name Hilton has a run-in with the law.

Programme code gone astray

The case of Sergey Aleynikov, a former programmer in the service of the investment bank Goldman Sachs, was not really proper espionage. He had stolen programme code and was pursued by the New York public prosecutor, who was quoted as saying that this programme code was as confidential as a "secret formula" (Lattmann 2012).

In this case, it was not known whether third parties were interested in the data or whether Aleynikov had perhaps offered it for sale. The importance given to company secrets by the court very clearly shows the significance that is nowadays ascribed to such immaterial values.

Sharp razors

The razor industry has a reputation for pursuing questionable pseudo-innovations. Following three blades, four or even five are now the measure of things – at least, that's the claim of the advertising of the few big providers, who oligopolistically dominate the market. Similar to trading in coffee capsules and printer cartridges, they sell their base equipment, in this case the razors, very cheaply in order to bring in margins which are all the higher with consumable parts, in other words the blades.

In the 1990s, there was a remarkable incident which demonstrates how times have changed in the business of illegally tapping company secrets: Steven Louis Davis, an employee of a supplier for the razor manufacturer Gillette, passed on confidential information to the competition. He faxed and mailed design drawings for a new razor to Warner-Lambert, Bic and American Safety Razor.

Davis was caught, charged and found guilty of the theft of business secrets and so-called wire fraud – in other words, fraud by telecommunication – which can attract a sentence of up to 20 years. According to several newspaper reports, Davis told the court that he had stolen the information out of anger over his line manager and fear of losing his job. It was a typical case of an unreflected act of revenge by a dissatisfied employee and an early case in which e-mails played a role in committing the offence.

Garbage bin archaeology

A ton of paper waste can be worth up to US$12,000 – at least when it involves espionage between companies. According to media reports, Investigative Group International, a detective agency hired by Oracle, had offered as much to cleaning staff who were in the process of dutifully disposing of paper waste from Microsoft. The head of Oracle, Larry Ellison, who was caught in the act, claimed that he regarded it as his public duty to uncover what he considered to be Microsoft's scandalous financing practises. In addition, the detective agency allegedly collected discrediting information on Bill Gates. The background to the "research" was antitrust proceedings against Microsoft (Markoff 2000).

This case shows what classical methods which are still regarded as legal are often still used to spy on competitors. Known as dumpster diving or rubbish archaeology, potentially relevant information is fished out of the opponent's waste. It may well be that a little money changes hands to facilitate direct access to the waste bins in the process. Incidentally, this case also casts some light on normal business practises in American and presumably also other companies.

Alden Taylor of the New York detective agency Kroll Associates stated in *USA Today* that almost all American top 500 companies had their own departments for spying on competitors (cited in *Manager Magazine*). In his opinion, economically motivated espionage was most widespread in Silicon Valley. According to Taylor, this generally involved spying out profit margins and project details. He stressed that this was done legally in most cases and that illegal acts were rare. What Taylor described here is more or less what is known as competitive intelligence (CI). It can safely be assumed that as the representative of a service provider in this segment he would tend to downplay any illegal activities.

Between garbage bins and false identities

They also fight with the gloves off on the shampoo front. In September 2001, *Fortune* magazine reported that Proctor & Gamble (P&G) had allegedly spied on its competitor Unilever (Fortune 2001). The target of the espionage activities was the hair care market.

Proctor & Gamble allegedly paid around US$3 million for dumpster diving. Agents of the company had masqueraded as market analysts and journalists in order to gain access to information. According to the *Fortune* magazine report, several documents with detailed plans for the further development of the hair care business in three years, including data on launch plans, prices and profit margins were allegedly collected during these activities (Fortune 2001).

This action not only infringed internal P&G guidelines but was above all an example of overstepping the mark in CI activities. According to the *New York Times*, Procter & Gamble had to pay US$10 million in compensation to Unilever (New York Times 2001).

Unfair play

Sport, specifically professional sport, also often involves large sums of money. Whether it's the Champions League or Formula One, the top events in all kinds of sport which reach a wide public have long been dominated by economic considerations. It is therefore no surprise that there is also an inclination here to examine the competitor's current state of development a little more closely. As is to be expected, there may be espionage wherever technology has a say in the outcome of a sporting event.

Secret formula

Formula One has therefore been through a whole series of espionage cases and subsequent arguments – McLaren against Ferrari, Red Bull against McLaren, Toyota against Ferrari or Team Shadow against Team Arrows. Racing history is full of accusations and cases of espionage which date back to the 1970s. The gains in know-how mainly involved development engineers who move from one racing stable to another. Toyota's motor racing department in Cologne was even searched in 2003 following accusations made by Ferrari as a result of an employee who changed jobs (Henry 2003).

Ferrari was also involved in an espionage affair in 2007. Documents from Ferrari reached McLaren – by courier. They were sent by a Ferrari chief developer, who obviously wanted a job with McLaren. Whether and to what extent the documents sent were actually used was never clarified. McLaren accepted the penalty payment of US$100 million imposed by the motorsport association (Henry 2003).

But despite this record fine, things just wouldn't settle down in Formula One. In 2011, for example, Red Bull made accusations of spying against McLaren: the bone of contention was the design of an exhaust system. The result is still unresolved today (Dunker 2011).

It is not only motorsport, in which everything depends on vehicle technology, which is threatened by spying by the competition: other types of sport repeatedly make the headlines with cases of espionage. For example, the Americas Cup sailing competition is sensitised to this kind of problem and has anchored in its statutes that no team may approach any other team closer than 200 metres without permission. But in 2012, the Oracle team came closer and a significant penalty was handed down: surrender of all photos taken during the approach, cancellation of five training days and a fine of US$15,200 (Bolle 2013). The latter was presumably just petty cash for software millionaire Larry Ellison's sailing team. However, the more serious part of the penalty was probably the loss of five days' training.

The Tour de France Trojan

Things are especially unsporting in cycling. This is the impression you get if you observe the scene for any length of time due to the regular cases of doping.

An especially blatant case in which the means used points to the future compared to other cases of unsporting espionage involved hacking into a doping laboratory in France.

The history of the case: in 2006, the American cycling professional Floyd Landis won the Tour de France, but after a positive dope test the title was taken away from him again. Landis proclaimed his innocence and went to court against the ban until he finally admitted having doped in 2009 (Clueley 2011). The interesting thing about the story was that a Trojan, which was discovered at the end of 2006 in the computer system of the doping laboratory which had found Landis out, had evidently purposefully stolen information on the case. Who had set the Trojan on the laboratory is still unknown today. However, the stolen information turned up at the trial against Floyd Landis and was intended to exculpate him; the intention was to show that the laboratory had been negligent (Jolly 2010).

How the documents came into Landis's possession was never explained. However, in 2009 a computer specialist from France named Alain Quiros, who also played an inglorious role in other espionage cases – for example the hacking of Greenpeace computers on behalf of EDF, the world's largest operator of nuclear power stations – admitted the Trojan attack on the laboratory. No connection to Landis could ever be proven, although a number of things indicated that it was a contract job (Clueley 2011).

Long live sport

However, it is not just sports with close relations to material and technique which are interesting from the point of view of espionage. In American football, the New England Patriots team came under suspicion of espionage in 2007: they had secretly video recorded the signals of the opposing defence and analysed it for their own benefit – doubtless no exception in this or any other sport in which tactics play an important role.

It is no wonder then that the mass sport of football is affected by spying. The German newspaper *Augsburger Allgemeine* reported on the 2007 women's football world championship in which Chinese men allegedly eavesdropped on the Danish women's team meeting. The Chinese were also accused of having organised systematic noise in front of the Danish team's hotel the night before the game. These accusations could not be proved, so the Fédération Internationale de Football Association, better known as "FIFA", shelved the accusations after thorough investigation (AA 2007). Beyond spying, the deliberate disturbance or harassment of competitors is also a core element in many sectors in the battle for first place. One last case concerned the theft of a notebook in 2008 which belonged to the president of FC Barcelona after bugs had been discovered in his office shortly beforehand. At the time, the press assumed that a competitor was involved. However, it was presumably less the game strategy and rather more the conditions of sponsoring agreements and television rights. After all, professional sport is a business almost like any other.

Varied interests

Spies are not only attracted by typical business secrets such as production methods or calculation schemes. In many cases, scientific curiosity is directed towards highly specific internal matters.

Perfectionist product counterfeiters

One does not necessarily expect industrial espionage to be behind counterfeit brand-name products. Strolling through the markets or watching street vendors plying their wares whilst on holiday, you may well see products which look very similar to well-known brands. Sometimes you could almost be inclined to believe a T-shirt or handbag is an original if the circumstances in which it is being promoted and the price invoked weren't dubious. Often the connoisseur can see blatant differences to the original, for example when the creativity of the forgers results in completely new variants of the product such as Rolex brand wristwatches which don't actually exist in the official catalogue. One can imagine how such items are made – mostly copied from the original goods or when an external assembly line finishes an order and then produces a few thousand more copies which are then marketed via dubious channels.

But what about high-tech products like mobile phones? Leaving aside "surplus production", copying such products is highly complex. This makes a case which became public in 2006 all the more astounding. According to reports in the *Helsingin Sanomat* newspaper (Helsingin Sanomat 2006), Finnish customs officials found a consignment of Nokia 1100 mobile phones where the packaging and transport route were suspicious but the phones were not immediately identifiable as forgeries. This led to some disconcertion amongst genuine customers as they feared their phones could therefore also be forgeries.

It was above all the quality of the counterfeit phones which was surprising in this case. Knowing that a number of test devices for mobile phones had also been stolen from Nokia (Suhl 2006) puts things in a different light: it is then probable that it was precisely these counterfeiters who stole the devices to ensure the quality of their phones. In a way, they made history by opening a new chapter on quality amongst forged products.

The short route to a new design

This was one of the big headlines in 1996. Following a long investigation, VW's corporate security succeeded in finding the loophole through which new designs were slipping to competitors and also to motoring magazines as prototypes. After photos which appeared in the press helped to identify the concern's own difficult-to-observe test track as the location for the pictures, a search for mini-cameras was initiated amongst the concern's own employees – without success.

Finally, they made an interesting discovery buried in a mound of earth: a technically highly developed camera with an infrared sensor and a satellite connection. The infrared sensor served as the shutter button as it was activated by the heat of a car within the angle of view of the camera. The pictures were immediately transferred to an unknown destination via the satellite connection.

According to VW, they suffered losses of hundreds of millions of euros (BZ 1996). It is not known whether the case was ever completely solved. However, the major technical effort involved definitely indicates a professional background.

The senior executive and the baby monitor

It was the night before a VW supervisory board meeting. Wendelin Wiedeking, the then-head of Porsche, was staying at the grand Ritz-Carlton hotel in Wolfsburg, conveniently almost directly in the concern grounds of "Golfsburg", as the town is jokingly known. The next morning, the Porsche security service found a switched-on baby monitor in his suite, as various media reported (Stern 2007).

Regular readers of the economics section of the press will remember that at the time the incident happened in November 2007, there was a skirmish in progress for dominance within the VW concern – an explosive situation. Although a security guard was suspected of having planted the device in Wiedeking's room and was charged, the real organisers remain unknown to the present day. An attempt by Wiedeking to set a trap for the culprit also failed, as was reported by the Porsche press office: "He made a number of statements in his room in order to see where they resurfaced" (FAZ 2008).

This was a good example of turning end consumer technologies into espionage tools, even if the originators have remained invisible to the present day and will possibly never be discovered.

Unsafe at any speed

It's not always the competition which can become dangerous. Often, companies also see other groups as a threat for their activities and attempt to influence or spy on them in order to better understand their motives or also to discredit opponents. Just such a case from the United States is almost legendary.

Consumer lawyer Ralph Nader, author of a book on the American automotive industry tellingly titled *Unsafe at Any Speed*, in which he accused the Chevrolet Corvair of being an unsafe design, thus attracted the attention of a private detective agency employed by GM. According to various media reports (History 1966), they also searched through his private life for weak points which they could use to discredit his person and thus also his mission.

However, the result was not in the interests of the company. The Corvair model was discontinued in 1969 following the bad press caused by Nader's book and numerous court cases brought by consumers due to inadequate product safety. Statutory standards for product safety, including compulsory safety belts for all passengers, were introduced into the US automobile industry, which to date is still little regulated. In the longer term, this development initiated competition for safe car concepts, which is definitely in the interests of auto-mobile manufacturers and ultimately of us all.

The notebook in the hotel room

Jens Kyllönen is one of the stars in a dazzling industry: he is a professional poker player. In 2012, he allegedly earned US$2.5 million playing poker. Whilst participating in a poker event in Barcelona, he found his notebook was missing on returning to his hotel room. When he returned later to his hotel room, it was miraculously back where it belonged.

Kyllönen, who immediately became suspicious, made some enquiries of the antivirus provider F-Secure and had his computer checked over. And they did actually find something: a remote access Trojan had been installed. With this, it would have been easy for a competitor to spy on Kyllönen whilst playing online poker. According to the security company, this was not the first case of a spying attack on a poker professional (F-Secure 2013).

A new age of industrial espionage

From eavesdroppers behind the door to wireless radio bugs – that would be a fair summary of the first phase of development for company espionage. In fact, technical developments have always led to the development of technical spying measures. The most common were and are:

- The use of wired eavesdropping equipment, known as bugs, to listen in on land-line phone calls and the use of disguised radio bugs;
- Bugging operations from outside through the use of directional micro-phones and laser directional microphones with which even conversations in enclosed spaces can be eavesdropped on from a distance;
- Software attacks on telecommunications equipment, especially telephone systems.
- The analysis of monitor radiation and other technical devices;
- The use of structure-borne sound transmitters.

Bugs, which are available in various shapes and sizes, are a classic. They are attached or built into presents, flowers and pot plants, mirrors, various items of office equipment, smoke alarms, furniture, kitchen appliances, wall clocks, air conditioning equipment, phones, mobile phones, computers, printers, faxes, copiers, curtains, carpet rails, partition walls, ceilings and many more. There have even been reports of bugging equipment in water kettles, which were apparently installed in the factory in China (Sharwood 2013). In short, imagination has no boundaries here.

The interception of radio signals is meanwhile also a major issue. This includes:

- Bugging wireless speech communications including cordless (DECT) phones, mobile phones, satellite phones, private mobile radio, radio micro-phones and so forth;

- Intercepting radio applications in information technology, including Wi-Fi, Bluetooth and so forth.

It has been observed for a number of years that specialist literature and components for building bugging equipment are becoming increasingly available. So-called spy shops in United Kingdom and abroad, including a number of web shops, have surveillance electronics on offer. Online marketplaces like eBay are also turning into trading centres for espionage equipment. Even sophisticated bugging equipment which was once only available to intelligence services is freely available online nowadays. In other words, technical attack methods are becoming popular whilst personal attacks which dominated the early age of industrial espionage are declining.

4 Economic and industrial espionage in the digital age

"Never before in the history of mankind has access to information been so quick and simple." The American information technologist Vinton Cerf, who is regarded as one of the fathers of the Internet, nicely sums up the big promise of the Internet age. The following examples, which would have been totally impossible or at least not possible in this form without the Internet, show that simplified access to information and universal networking can have risky side effects.

Helpless victims

Digital transformation doesn't stop at industrial espionage. With new technologies, it is becoming increasingly easy to access data without authorisation. Unlike in earlier times, it is often no longer necessary to be physically present: with suitable software, you can attack a target company in any other country. This is possible because of the universal networking of our world. Moreover, many of these attacks remain undiscovered for a long time. When such an attack is finally uncovered, the victims are often left with nothing more than a feeling of helplessness.

The author and the Trojan Horse

The Israeli author Amnon Jackont thought it must be a private feud when he discovered in 2005 that individual chapters of his as-yet-unpublished book *L Is for Lies* had turned up in online literary forums and had been harshly criticised. A Wikipedia article about him was also manipulated, and private e-mails and other documents inexplicably found their way onto the Internet (Frankel 2005).

Jackont suspected it was an act of revenge. He told police he suspected that his wife's former son-in-law, the computer specialist Michael Haephrati, now wanted revenge against him after his divorce and had infiltrated his computer with a virus. In fact, Jackont's computer was actually nothing more than a small side-show in a wide-ranging espionage scandal in Israel. However, Jackont's suspicions about the originator were not wrong: Haephrati had indeed written a piece of malware which could not be detected by the virus scanners of the time which he had sold to a number of detective agencies.

As the police investigations under Operation Horserace discovered, Volvo's importer was spying on Champion Motors, Volkswagen's representative in Israel. Yes, the satellite television operator, stole the customer lists of the cable network operator Hot. The mobile phone operators Cellcom and Pelephone spied on the computers of their competitor Orange. The list is long and full of well-known names. The best-known large Israeli companies, department store chains and vendors of mineral water, food manufacturers and computer companies were all named as either victims or perpetrators (Sahm 2005). The malware was purposefully distributed via e-mail and on a presentation CD. In the case of Amnon Jackont, the infection apparently came from an anonymously sent CD-ROM with a book manuscript.

The most remarkable thing about this case was its commercial dimension. Michael Haephrati, who was living in London at the time, thus appeared to have worked as a service provider for the detective agencies and billed them for £3,500 for every initial infection of a target computer with the Trojan as well as a further £900 per month for access to confidential material. He was later sentenced to pay a compensation of NIS 400,000 to Amnon Jackont (Paraszczuk 2012). Overall, this spy software was allegedly installed at over 60 companies. As a result of investigations, 18 people were arrested in Israel, Great Britain and Germany (Sharvit 2005). A number of very well-known Israeli companies from a variety of sectors were involved in these activities.

After this incident, we can definitely assume that the phenomenon of "espionage as a service" exists and that it is mostly hidden behind legal-sounding names. There are also patterns of attack which are not detected by conventional security systems and under certain circumstances are purposefully tailored for individual recipients. What is also shocking is that the effort required for a successful attack, which makes use of the networked world's security vulnerabilities, has become very small whilst the effect can be enormous.

The price of support

The IT sector would not be conceivable without the associated service. For example, support websites offer help with setting up and operation, permit the downloading of updates and much more. In view of the short update cycles in this sector, economically meaningful marketing of software and software-based products, for example Blu-ray players, scanners, printers and mobile phones, is hardly conceivable without the associated support sites. Just imagine if every customer enquiry led to a long, drawn-out phone conversation for the provider, and every update made it necessary to send out CDs or other data carriers or to recall products for updates or improvements as is currently often still the case in the automotive industry.

In the area of commercial user software too – the German company SAP for example – support applications are indispensable. Typically, maintenance services are in demand – not always from the manufacturer themselves but often from specialist service companies. For example, the American company Oracle, whose databases are frequently used as a basis for SAP installations, is simultaneously a supplier and a competitor of SAP. In 2010, according to a study by RAAD Research, at least two thirds of all SAP systems contained an Oracle product as the database – which made SAP the biggest vendor of Oracle licences. In the view of market research, companies are thus partners on the one hand and arch-enemies on the other. SAP does a lot to cover this market share with their own products and thus to reduce dependence on Oracle, for example through the introduction of new database technologies.

An incident in which the Americans at Oracle accused the Germans at SAP of espionage must be seen against the background of this special competitive situation. SAP had bought the software company TomorrowNow and then downloaded data from Oracle support systems as an Oracle partner – with customers' access data. According to media reports, SAP emphasised the basic legality of this access by TomorrowNow, but spoke themselves of the "inappropriate manner" of the access (CNET 2007).

Whether this was really industrial espionage or a more or less authorised business interest remained open. In any case, an American court was of the opinion that Oracle was entitled to compensation from SAP and sentenced the German software company to record compensation of US\$1.3 billion (Reuters 2010). Following several rounds of proceedings, an out-of-court settlement was reached to the value of US\$306 million (ITPro 2012). All SAP statements and court decisions can still be accessed on a website set up by SAP at www.tnlawsuit.com.

A similar incident happened in Austria in 2016 where two companies – Axess and Skidata – battled over the market leadership for access control systems for ski regions and sports arenas. Axess sued Skidata for illegally harvesting customer data from their sites and using it to gain unfair advantage in competitive bids. Although this was initially turned down in court, it remains unclear whether there is some truth in it.

The main difference to the cases dealt with in the previous chapter is the dematerialisation of the collection of information: nobody had to travel to a foreign country for months or even years – quite the opposite. None of those involved even had to leave their desks to gain access to the documents. This even holds through in the case from Austria. Both companies' headquarters are a just a few miles away from each other but the alleged attack happened by electronic communication.

The trainee with the USB stick

Information cannot always be stolen from experts' computers via download or Trojan. Sometimes the classical data carrier is the first choice – really pretty obvious in the era of USB sticks and external hard disks.

A 22-year-old Chinese trainee at the French automotive supplier Valeo was regarded as being outstandingly talented, with several degrees and a fluent knowledge of several languages. She stood out at her workplace for her exaggeratedly high motivation (China 2005). When her apartment was searched in

April 2005, several computers and hard disks with data on Valeo products were found, including data which was confidential because it belonged to vehicles which were not even on the market at the time (FT 2005). Some two years after the incident, the overzealous Chinese employee was sentenced to one year in prison with ten months suspended.

What was interesting was that – as several newspapers reported – the young woman denied accusations of spying and declared in interrogations that the company computer had been full so she had copied part of the data and stored it on her own computer. Somebody should perhaps have been surprised at an applicant with especially fitting qualifications. There are indeed indications that CVs are frequently manipulated to get a job in the target company.

The pattern of attack is always an ideal qualification for the job advertised. Even if it has to be stated that there is no concrete evidence as to the culprit, it is obvious that it was probably state-sponsored players acting for a certain giant Eastern empire.

The China-critical *China Intern* website assumes that China also has a well-structured espionage network in Germany and other countries (China 2005):

> The lowest levels are students. The responsible agents amongst the students have to report to the consulate responsible for them once a month to report all important events to their handlers; the consulate in Bonn is, for example, responsible for Cologne and Munich is responsible for the technologically especially important region of Nuremberg, etc.

There are similar reports to be found in other sources such as the *Epoch Times*, an international magazine with its main focus on China. It confirms the systematic approach and the control by the embassies with reference to a former consulate employee: according to this source, a large number of students do this for love of their country and develop no sense of wrongdoing (Epoch 2007). If you ask Chinese officials about such practises, they deny them profusely. As with other sources on the theme of espionage against companies, the veracity of the statements quoted cannot be verified.

The pattern of attack, taking everything that can be taken on a data carrier, is definitely not an isolated case. The easy availability of data carriers makes it easy to steal data.

The classic hack

As the security software company McAfee, a subsidiary of the processor manufacturer Intel, discovered in 2011, internal information had been stolen by hackers from six American and European oil companies including ExxonMobil, Shell and BP (McAfee 2011). Documents lost contained information on oil and gas fields, including quotations for financing. According to the InGuardians security company, these were mainly topographical maps which were intended to assist with the development of oil reserves – and which were worth millions of dollars.

The attacks, which were given the name Night Dragon, began back in November 2009 and were presumably mainly controlled from China. The remarkable thing about them were the multistage nature of these attacks: first, servers in the extranet, which were accessible from outside, were attacked and then subsequently internal targets attacked via them. Individual employees were also targeted with individually produced software. The target was company servers in the United States and the Netherlands. In a detailed analysis of operation Night Dragon, McAfee reported that attacks also took place on individual persons and management in Taiwan, Greece and Kazakhstan. It stated in the appendix of this white paper (McAfee 2011):

> We [McAfee] assume that numerous actors were involved in the attacks. We were able to identify one as an individual who was not necessarily directly involved but provided major parts of the infrastructure for the attack. The person is located in the city of Heze in the province of Shandong in China.

McAfee also assumed that this person was connected to but not necessarily the main mastermind of the attacks, as they had provided rented servers in the United States which played a major role in the attacks. The fact that one of the main features of the systems was that they provided no log files and therefore no records of system activities was a further original detail.

In this document, McAfee also stated further evidence that the attacks were of Chinese origin, including the spelling of certain passwords and also the use of IP addresses from the Beijing area as well as hacker tools from underground Chinese forums. The discovery that all attacks took place between 09:00 and 17:00 local Beijing time was also interesting. This analysis also made clear how difficult it is sometimes for security experts to attribute attacks to a particular attacker or even just a particular country.

For whom the sun shines

The SolarWorld company virtually represents both the rise and fall of the solar industry in Europe. And like many other companies, SolarWorld was a victim of Chinese espionage. According to a report by *Foreign Policy* (Harris 2014), Chinese military hackers invaded computers of SolarWorld's American subsidiary and stole important internal company information, in particular information on pricing and marketing strategies. The company was first made aware of this attack by the FBI in July 2012 and immediately tightened up its security measures.

The especially interesting thing about this case is that the spies were apparently interested in correspondence between SolarWorld and the lawyers who were representing the company in a trade dispute with China (Harris 2014), for there is considerable competition amongst spies to target the entire renewable energies industry. Trade disputes can always become a motivator for state protagonists to explore the opposing side's main structures. Especially because companies see themselves as potential targets for competitor espionage and tighten up their IT security accordingly, it is often their service providers such as lawyers, tax advisors and auditors which are spied on as they are easier targets from which to obtain confidential information.

Medium-sized companies in the sights of hackers

With 44 employees and around €5 million in turnover, Clearaudio is a typical German medium-sized company ("*Mittelstand*") and sustains its position in a highly competitive sector with innovations for the consumer electronics market. Clearaudio specialises in high-quality record players and is regarded as a leading innovator, for example with a sophisticated magnetic bearing which guarantees vibration-free record playing and thus better sound quality. Around two years of work and an investment of €350,000 went into the development of this bearing.

Much to everyone's surprise, when devices with this innovative bearing were first presented at a trade exhibition in Munich, there was a record player with an identically designed bearing a few booths away – from a Chinese manufacturer. Clearaudio's design plans had apparently been stolen in an attack on their company server. Fortunately, the company succeeded in having the Chinese imports stopped with the assistance of German customs.

Clearaudio is one of the few companies which talks openly about the incident – and by no means an exception. In the estimation of German government officials, namely the North Rhine-Westphalian Office for the Protection of the Constitution, most cases of technology theft happen to small- and medium-sized companies (Kopplin 2011).

Whether this holds true in other countries is unclear since the studies that can be found are difficult to compare.

The hacker and the network

At the beginning of 2005, a 26-year-old Hungarian was sentenced to three years in prison in Sweden for industrial espionage. The IT consultant had infiltrated the intranet of the telecommunications supplier Ericsson, which operates internationally but is based in Sweden, and had spied on company secrets for a period of several months (Demsteader 2005). Online news service *Heise online* reported extensively on the case (Heise 2005):

> In March 2002, the man who has become known in the Swedish press as the Ericsson Spy gained access to Ericsson's global network and began to explore it thoroughly. [. . .] By means of Trojan horses installed with users and further programmes, he penetrated ever deeper into the computer network and was initially successful in covering his tracks. Until his arrest in October 2004, he copied a large number of secret documents including the source code for Sony Ericsson mobile phones. In interrogations, Csaba Richter described security at Ericsson as pretty lax.

According to the media report quoted, the attacks were made from home: Csaba Richter's parents' house was the starting point for the attacks in which not only internal Ericsson information but also Swedish armed forces' military secrets were copied. In court, he stated that he had had no intention of causing damage but wanted a job with Ericsson. However, his assertions were contradicted by the fact that he had offered the stolen data for sale online.

He was arrested with the help of the Swedish secret service, Säkerhetspolisen (SÄPO), which Ericsson had called on for assistance. No further details of the break-in and the trial are known as the case was placed under a 20-year information ban – a rare occurrence in Sweden, a country which is normally very open.

This attack exhibited all the typical characteristics: it was made via the Internet, remained undiscovered for a long time and an enormous amount of information was syphoned off. What was missing was an initial motive, otherwise the culprit wouldn't have offered what he'd stolen for sale online but would have remained invisible after the theft – and the incident would perhaps only have been discovered much later, if at all.

Plundered into insolvency

It was all over by the beginning of 2009. The Canadian Nortel Corporation, one of the globally leading network equipment suppliers, had to declare bankruptcy after over 100 years of company history and also right in the middle of an Internet boom, which actually meant lots of business for all suppliers.

Somewhat later it became known that Nortel had been spied on for years. Seven passwords stolen from Nortel managers in 2000 had sufficed to gain access to important development documents, business plans and e-mails. The break-in was not discovered until 2004, but the passwords were simply changed. Espionage software anchored deep on the system was initially overlooked and an internal investigation was abandoned after six months. Nortel didn't take the problem seriously enough, and so the attacks continued unhindered for the next few years (Whitney 2012). The former Nortel security advisor wrote the following on his LinkedIn page (LinkedIn 2017):

> My efforts found advanced persistent intruders in our corporate network at Nortel. I proved system compromises where our AV guru was unable to find anything wrong. The intruder(s) had complete control of internal systems from the Internet and had an encrypted tunnel likely for Command and Control.

Even if all traces point to China, it is still not clear today who was ultimately behind the attacks on Nortel (Gorman 2012).

What is frightening about this case is not just the ignorance with which management faced the problem. It is above all frightening that it was a company in a sector in which it could be assumed that they were aware of the importance of network security. In addition, it becomes clear how carelessly passwords were bypassed in practise and how negligent it was not to take additional security measures such as two-factor authentication.

Spied on and repelled

From a network equipment provider to a telecommunications concern, the Norwegian Telenor company suffered an attack similar to that on Nortel which was discovered at the beginning of 2013. The company itself reported the incident to the Norwegian criminal investigation department and informed the HSM national security authority and the cyber-counterintelligence service Cyberforsvaret (News 2013).

The personal computers of senior company managers were the target of the attack. What was particularly interesting in this case was that the security problems were discovered by the Telenor Security Operation Centre. The centre had noticed unusual data traffic from management computers and had investigated. According to media reports, around 20 members of staff worked on surveillance of this unusual Internet traffic between the company and the outside world and discovered that the attack weapon was prepared e-mails which brought in Trojans piggyback-style and appeared to come from known contacts, and partly even from colleagues within the company. The precise targets of the attackers and their identity are not known in this case. However, the security representative had to admit that the attackers had been in a position to steal internal company information.

This case is unusual in that a leading telecommunications company became the target of hacker attacks. The measures initiated by Telenor at least meant that the attack was not only discovered but also ultimately successfully repelled.

In this case Telenor itself was the target of corporate espionage efforts. With the increasing usage of telecommunications infrastructures and cloud services by businesses worldwide, telecommunications and IT service companies will be attacked more and more to get hold of the company secrets of their customers.

Designed and collected

Just imagine: for months, your employees have been working on the design of a revolutionary new product with AutoCAD, one of the most widespread applications for producing technical drawings. As soon as everything has been finished, you attempt to apply for a patent. But this is rejected because someone in China was faster than you – a nightmare which could by all means come true.

In 2012, the security researchers at ESET discovered malware which was able to steal documents produced with AutoCAD and send them to China. What was even worse was that according to ESET analyses, tens of thousands of design drawings had already been copied in this way and sent to e-mail addresses with Chinese Internet providers (Rubenking 2012). Every newly created design was automatically passed on by the ACAD/Medre AutoCAD worm, as it is called by security researchers, which is designed to do just that. In the opinion of the security experts, the computer worm's approach was not particularly complex: it changed an AutoCAD start file and thus gained control of the programme.

ESET emphasised that ACED/Medre could be switched off and that Chinese providers which operate the e-mail addresses received were cooperative in ending the attacks. However, it must be assumed that many similar attacks remain undiscovered. Compared with the approach of personally worming oneself in and copying documents described in the preface, this example clearly shows what a technological change we are experiencing, particularly in the field of industrial espionage. Unlike 20 years ago, it is neither necessary nor expedient for the attacker to drop by in person, which is risky, as long as suitable malware can be put in place.

Operation Aurora

One of the most elaborate attacks ever brought to light was known under the name of Aurora. This is remarkable not only because Google was a main target but also above all due to its great complexity, which indicated the high professionalism of the team of attackers.

At the beginning of 2010, Google published a statement on its official blog, according to which the company had been subject to attacks originating from China along with around 20 other firms in various sectors (Google 2010). It was initially assumed that Google's activities in China were to be affected and that political matters were the main motivation, because the mailboxes of human rights activists who were active in China were targeted. It was actually primarily about stealing intellectual property from Google, Adobe and other companies in a much more concerted action than had ever been seen before. A total of 34 companies were attacked, including financial sector, arms manufacturing and other companies from many other sectors, for example Dow Chemical, Northrop Grumman, Symantec, Yahoo! and the web host Rackspace (Jackson 2010). The hackers were particularly interested in stealing source code. According to a report by *Wired* magazine, they exploited a so-called zero-day security leak in the ubiquitous Adobe Reader programme (Wired 2010a).

According to the iDefense security company, which was referenced in the *Wired* article, the attackers sent e-mails to previously spied-out addresses with a manipulated PDF file attached. A Trojan known as Trojan.Hydraq installed itself and then waited for commands from a control server if these files were clicked. What was especially remarkable was the ability of the attackers not only to successfully attack the right people in the company and to get them to click the attachments sent by means of cleverly forged e-mails but also to find security loopholes which were not yet known to conventional security software.

According to iDefense, Google source code was one of the targets of the attacks. However, it was of little surprise that Google did not want to comment and that an Adobe speaker also refused to answer questions about whether source code had been stolen. The behaviour already familiar from other cases was repeated here, namely only to admit what was absolutely unavoidable and already known in case of security breaches.

In April of the same year, the *New York Times* reported – quoting a Google insider – on the actual extent and strategic goal of the attacks (Markoff 2010a). Apparently, the target was indeed a core piece of Google's technology, the central password management system, which is known under the name of Gaia. The theft of the Gaia code started with a targeted message to a Google employee in China via Microsoft Messenger, an instant messaging system. By means of a click on a link, the attacked user accessed a site infected with malware, and their computer became a gateway for the attackers to gain access to the computers of a group of software developers at Google headquarters via this compromised computer system. The attackers' real target was located there: a software repository, a server on which a team of developers' source code was stored.

Further details are just as interesting. The control servers were apparently operated by a regular hosting provider in the United States (Paul 2010) – not unusual for such attacks. However, it was possible to trace the source of the attacks back to two Chinese training establishments by means of IP addresses: the elite Shanghai Jiaotong University, which is known for its especially good information technology training, and also the Lanxiang Vocational School. This special vocational school is suspected of training computer experts for the Chinese military; at any rate, it was set up with the support of the military. And the students at Jiaotong University are anything but average: shortly before, they had won the Battle of the Brains programming competition organised by IBM – ahead of teams from top American universities such as Stanford (Markoff 2010b).

According to the report in the *New York Times*, there was disagreement amongst security experts about the evaluation of the findings. Whilst some assumed that the training establishments served as cover organisations for the Chinese authorities, others believed the attacks could also come from a third country or were simply intended to cover up large-scale industrial espionage activity. That would imply that the attacks on the e-mail accounts of human-rights campaigners about Operation Aurora were simply a diversionary tactic.

The thing to remember is that even outstandingly well-set-up organisations like Google can do little against a concerted attack. And the problem of attributing such massive attacks also remains unsolved in such sophisticated scenarios.

New hazard potentials

It has already become clear in several of the examples given that just the improved availability of long-familiar technologies alone can already be enough to conjure up new potential hazards. However, the all-too-human element can help to make the breakthrough. It is worth looking at how small the difference between espionage and sabotage is and how variable the motives of attackers are.

Dangerous places and devices

How dangerous is an Internet café? What risk can a smartphone charger represent? Technical progress makes a reassessment of numerous apparently familiar places and devices necessary and also supplies completely new areas of activity for spies with drones and wearables.

The return of the dreaded copier

Contrary to expectations, the copier as described in Chapter 3 has not fallen into disuse as a spying tool. Quite the opposite: the further technical development from copying systems to multifunctional printers opens up completely new possibilities for spies. Such systems often contain hard disks which serve as temporary storage for printing and copying jobs. The print files are sometimes stored for months on end. Such a system can therefore contain extremely interesting information for a spy.

Once the type of printing system used by a company has been determined, impersonating a maintenance technician is really simple. He "officially" installs an urgently needed update and of course also replaces the hard disk while he's at it – the friendly service technician always carries a few free replacement parts. This terribly simple attack is effective even today. Common providers of multifunctional printers have recognised the problem, but they only offer solutions for securing the problem, for example encrypting the storage system, at extra cost – extra costs which many companies are happy to save.

This obvious approach is just one of many conceivable attacks on modern printing systems. As has been demonstrated by security researchers, it is also possible to manipulate the software of certain printer types to progressively permit more access: print jobs can be diverted so that the attackers always automatically receive a copy without the user noticing a thing. Printers which have been manipulated in this way can also be extended to become advanced spying units to attack other computer systems in the network of the company being spied on.

The possibility of destroying a printer should also be mentioned: in laboratory tests it proved possible to set the paper on fire via a laser printer's heating wire – sabotage instead of espionage. Salvatore Stolfo, a professor at Columbia University in New York, and one of his PhD students succeeded in demonstrating this kind of access using various Hewlett-Packard (HP) printers back in 2011 (Columbia 2011).

This could be dismissed as a purely theoretical hazard, but the shocking thing about it is that direct access to the printer itself is not necessary in order to install a dangerous update because the printer types investigated regularly check online whether a firmware update is available. Unbelievably, the origin of the file is not verified so that any document with additional malware attached is enough to take control of the printer (Antony 2011). In principle, a prepared file sent to an employee on some pretext would be enough. The printer would then be hijacked as soon as this is printed out.

The hazards described here are not limited to HP printers but basically exist for all devices which can be provided with new operating software without any further security measures. Something as simple as a print job may not suffice in all cases as with HP, but this risk still exists everywhere, for there is no security software to prevent it. A compromised printer is not recognisable as such to a user in the company.

Modern multifunctional printers also have further functions which can be of interest to hackers. I know of security researchers who can manipulate printers for home use so that they hand over internal data to the outside via built-in Wi-Fi functionality even if the company network itself is highly secure. Because modern printer systems are basically small computers which contain extensive computer functionality and are used to print or scan internal company documents, they will certainly become a favourite playground for attackers in the future.

The curse of the good deed

Data can be lost in totally unexpected ways. Whoever donates old computers to social institutions should know that simply deleting or formatting the hard disk alone does not prevent sensitive data which was stored on the device from falling into the wrong hands. The same applies if the devices are handed over for recycling. In 2013, a student who I commissioned for this experiment succeeded in getting hold of 20 retired company PCs from the recycling centre of a German university town within just a few weeks. Of these, two still contained internal documents of local corporations which were still legible in plain text, and in a further six cases it was possible to reconstitute the apparently deleted data without problems. All he did was just ask in a friendly way.

Some years before, in 2001, I acquired a storage system for my company from a liquidator who was winding up a well-known Internet company for a Munich-based insolvency administrator – a hard disk system with an unheard-of number of terabytes of storage. Unbelievably, the hard disks were still full of e-mails from numerous private persons and also companies from all over Germany. One could say that this company had nothing more to fear as it had already gone bust, but ultimately this was their customers' confidential data which was easy for third parties to find.

A good alternative to a trip to the recycling centre or the insolvency administrator is eBay. By its own admission, the Pointsec company succeeded in reconstructing data on 70 out of 100 hard disks acquired from eBay (Point 2004). A targeted attack in this way is, of course, unlikely, as the storage systems are rarely sold directly by the company which formerly used them. It is perhaps statistically insignificant but still shocking because it can happen to anyone. In one particular case, it was possible to reconstruct client data from a tax advisory and auditing company which was found on the computer. No matter how perfect your own company's security system is, it is useless if a partner doesn't take good care of the data they are entrusted with.

It is, however, conceivable that a spy attack on a company could be started by pretending to be a representative of a charitable organisation. You just have to claim that you are collecting old PCs for a good cause, for example for senior citizens, disadvantaged young people or poor immigrants. In case of doubt, therefore, radical measures are the only option: remove and mechanically destroy the hard disks before handing over the computer.

Espionage via the power plug

According to the *Telegraph* newspaper, an especially odd case of competitor observation was allegedly carried out in 2013 in France by an Aachen-based engineering consulting company commissioned by BMW (Samuel 2013). The target was a car-sharing provider of electric vehicles with numerous stations in the Paris and Lyon areas. Unlike DriveNow, which is operated by BMW and Sixt and uses the free-floating model, Autolib only uses fixed locations for the cars and only one vehicle type: an electric vehicle built by the French concern in collaboration with Pininfarina, which is completely unknown outside France. The infrastructure and the fleet management are also proprietary developments.

According to media reports, technicians allegedly tapped into charging columns on behalf of BMW in order to obtain system information. BMW merely regarded the tests as compatibility tests. The staff of the engineering consultants were arrested temporarily and released after questioning. The timing of this news could hardly have been worse for BMW, as it occurred on almost precisely the same day as the start of the International Automobile Exhibition in Frankfurt. The burning question is whether it was really just an acceptable test or rather an attempt to obtain more information than mere plug compatibility. Or had the engineering consultants perhaps overstepped the mark?

Even if this case can be dismissed as a one-off incident, power plugs do play a role in other cases – as a source for targeted attacks on unsuspecting smartphone users. Anyone who uses their smartphone intensively is familiar with the problem: the day is far from over and the battery is already alarmingly low. Public charging stations, which are frequently found at airports and in stations, company foyers, coffee houses or in modern hotel rooms, are then a blessing. What is not generally known is what a risk they are for stored data, for it can also be copied from devices via the USB interface which is used for charging. It gets worse: stored data can be modified, deleted or overwritten and malware can be installed. It is enough to manipulate such a charging station or even to go the whole hog and provide your own prepared power supply.

Back in 2011, a security research team demonstrated the risks at the DEF CON hacker conference. More than 360 participants at the conference could not resist using charging stations, although the risks of local networks and other technical equipment were clearly described on the conference website. They used the free charging stations for their mobile phones which were installed as a showcase in order to point out the risks (Krebs 2011) There is already a specific term in English for this perfidious method of stealing data: "juice jacking".

The security researcher Jonathan Zdziarski pointed out in 2013 that correspondingly prepared iOS devices remain in contact with bugging equipment even after charging is finished and thus permit an attacker permanent access.

The reason for this is pairing, which, once initiated, permits wireless exchange. It is then enough to have used a charging station which is infected with a virus to ruin the security of data stored on your own smartphone.

The best protection against such threats is therefore always only to use your own charger. It also makes sense to have a backup battery. Switching off the phone before charging does not always help: depending on the model, access to stored data is still possible, or the phone is automatically rebooted on connection to the power supply such as is the case with Windows smartphones. A special USB cable which does not permit data transfer but is sold purely as a charging cable can also be of use.

But you don't need to fumble around with hacking tools any longer. Israel-based company Cellebrite offers tools for "mobile forensics" which can be used intuitively if you can get a hold on physical device for some time.

On its corporate website as well as at large trade fairs (e.g. MWC, the Mobile World Congress, the biggest fair for mobile technology held every year in Barcelona, Spain), Cellebrite shows products for the physical extraction of mobile data.

The website lists what can be retrieved (Cellebrite 2015):

- intact and deleted passwords;
- installed applications;
- geo tags;
- location information;
- media files such as photos and videos taken by the user;
- GPS fixes;
- e-mails and chats.

Of course, Cellebrite markets its products and services only for government and law enforcement usage and has strong criteria on whom they are willing to sell to. As we know from other companies selling surveillance equipment, it is not impossible to get your hands on these devices even if you are not on the list of legitimate buyers.

The Internet café risk factor

In many regions of the world, Internet cafés are the first choice for Internet access. Sometimes these are the only option and definitely cheaper than data roaming with a mobile phone.

The temptation to access company data via Internet café computer systems, perhaps to quickly check your e-mails, is great. In the simplest of cases this means using an Internet browser to access the company's webmail portal. This is, however, highly dangerous, since such computers are often infected with malware, either by the operator themselves or other guests. A simple keylogger – a programme which records keyboard input – on such a publicly accessible computer is enough to pick up users' passwords. The careless user has absolutely no means of telling whether the system is infected with malware.

But danger not only lurks in dubious Internet cafés. The same applies to the guest PCs made available by many hotels, regardless of whether these are freely available as a service in the lobby or await paying customers in the hotel's own business centre.

Public Wi-Fi

Just like public charging stations, public network access points can contain considerable risks for smartphones, tablets and so forth and therefore for the company. A third party can always eavesdrop if the connection is not encrypted, and important passwords can then sometimes be seen in plain text. What was a serious problem some years ago is now not quite so risky because many services available via Internet themselves now offer encryption and thus an adequately secure environment even in public networks.

However, the trustworthiness of the network operator can remain questionable: in the course of Edward Snowden's revelations it became known that the Communications Security Establishment Canada (CSEC), the Canadian secret service, operates free Wi-Fi networks for travellers at Canadian airports. These serve as a starting point for tracking the location and movement radius of travellers over several weeks – then via Wi-Fi in hotels, coffee houses and so forth. Even if this does not cause any concrete economic damage, the location of a certain person alone can provide valuable details. Processes which aggregate movement and other metadata are thus potentially highly dangerous should the data fall into the wrong hands. And the fact that state intelligence services sometimes collaborate with private companies, as seen in the many examples in previous chapters, should be grounds enough to make business-people act prudently.

According to a blog post of Czech security company Avast, most people trust public Wi-Fi more than they should. To prove their point, they had bogus Wi-Fi access points set up at the 2016 Republican National Convention in Cleveland with phoney network names (SSIDs) like "Google Starbucks", "Xfinitywifi", "Attwifi", "I vote Trump! free Internet" and "I vote Hillary! free Internet". More than 1,000 people used these network traps and almost 70 percent exposed their identities when connected, while 44 percent checked their e-mails or chatted via messenger apps (Avast 2016).

Drones and espionage

Wikipedia states that the word "drone" originates from the Indo-European "*dhren*" (humming). What is meant here is not the male honeybee or wasp, which is normally associated with the term, but a more modern equivalent.

In the context of this book, drones are unmanned aviation systems which are typically associated with military technology. Some types of drones can navigate and fly autonomously whilst others require remote control by an operator on the ground who may be thousands of kilometres away. Autonomous flying means that a drone can fly certain missions completely without external intervention. Such drones take off, fly, perform certain operations in flight and land fully autonomously. Drones come in different sizes, from small systems or microdrones which are a just a few centimetres long, up to the size of an aeroplane. The Boeing Condor drone, for example, has a wingspan of over 60 metres. Drones are meanwhile flying all over the world: even North Korea, which is generally regarded as backwards, has such unmanned flying objects.

Amongst other things, drones are deployed for surveillance, for example by the military for reconnaissance or by the police for monitoring demonstrations and events. Depending on requirements, they can be equipped with high-quality cameras and sensors or also weapons systems. The public debate on drones is therefore strongly influenced by the targeted killing of suspected terrorists by the United States in third-world countries such as Pakistan. There are numerous more or less meaningful uses beyond military and police organisations.

These flying devices became known to a wide cross-section of the public as the online shop operator Amazon announced that it wanted to deliver packages with drones in the future. The service, known as Amazon Prime Air, was to deliver packages in record time – 30 minutes after placing an order. Amazon's boss Jeff Bezos emphasised the seriousness of these ambitions. Even if you dismiss Amazon making deliveries by drone as a public relations gag, the public perception of the drone system profited enormously from it – worldwide. It was no wonder that several logistic companies like DHL and UPS test delivered packages by drone.

One of the drones used by DHL flew over an Alpine pass, autonomously overcoming an altitude difference of more than 1,600 metres. According to the website of the drone maker Microdrones, it can remain in the air with a payload of 1.2 kilogrammes in adverse conditions (minus 20 to plus 50 degrees Celsius) for up to 88 minutes and is rain proof and dust resistant. Microdrones lists aerial photography, aerial video recording, industrial inspection and various surveillance tasks as possible uses, explicitly including surveillance of critical infrastructures – not necessarily one's own if you are a spy.

It is not only professional drones that cost four or five-figure sums which are suitable for spying. These flying aerial devices have meanwhile reached the stage of being toys for adults. Searching Google for drones returns a number of providers. Kits or even more or less completely assembled drones can be bought for just a few hundred US dollars or euros. The French hands-free equipment manufacturer Parrot has several drones on offer: the AR.Drone2.0, for example, can be controlled by smartphone or tablet and costs less than €300 ready to fly in various online shops. Possible uses for this model, with just 10 to 12 minutes flight time per battery charge and control ability within Wi-Fi range, are pretty limited. But it should definitely suffice to take a peek over the fence at an automobile manufacturer's secret testing ground on the lookout for new vehicle models.

Repelling drones should be a high priority for companies for which they can be a real threat. Various companies are therefore already working on repulsing measures. A company has even turned up on the Kickstarter start-up financing platform, on which young entrepreneurs seek financing for their developments, which wants to offer a kind of alarm system against unwanted visits by drones. How this is to be realised from a technical point of view was not clear from the published tender. But what is certain is that with the further spread of drone systems, research-oriented companies will need some kind of antidrone firewall.

Mind the camera

It is an inseparable part of our conception of espionage: the pocket camera for inconspicuously photographing construction plans and industrial plants. The legendary Minox miniature cameras, known to spy movie fans of James Bond films such as *On Her Majesty's Secret Service* from 1969, left an enduring impression with entire generations.

The inventor of Minox cameras, Walther Zapp, developed a camera with a picture format of 9 by 11 millimetres in 1936 – smaller than a cigar and lighter than a lighter, as it was described at the time – which went into production in 1938 and was built until 1995, constantly developed but still based on the original principle. It took decades until the rise of digital photography and the wide distribution of mobile phone cameras before new photo-technical developments came on the scene which changed the world of espionage. Meanwhile, really small digital cameras are available in every spy shop and are often built into everyday objects such as wristwatches, pocket calculators, radio alarm clocks or wall clocks. The simplest way to install these is to offer them to the company as promotional giveaways.

Another important development to do with camera technology, however, can be regarded as much more alarming: the mobile phone camera. Miniaturisation plays a major role here too. Photo cameras in mobile phones have been known in Japan since 1999 and have been available in Europe since about 2002. The first devices with a resolution of just 0.1 to 0.3 megapixels were hardly any use for anything, at least not for espionage. Meanwhile, just about every available mobile phone offers resolution of several megapixels. The Nokia Lumia frontrunner with 41 megapixels even had a unit which brought with it a lossless digital zoom with a picture size of 5 megapixels and produced amazingly high-quality photos. Twelve to sixteen megapixels are now standard on most smartphones; even cheap devices have a decent camera now. For videos, full HD recordings are also the standard almost everywhere. Top smartphones can often master the even higher ultra-high-definition (UHD) standard with 3,840 by 2,160 pixels, which is four times the pixel count for full HD with 1,920 by 1,080 megapixels.

The development of mobile phones into smartphones, which are practically always able to transmit content via a data connection, is just as remarkable as the trend towards ever higher-quality optics. Photos, and increasingly videos, can thus be transmitted immediately via mobile communications technology.

Smartphones as pocket bugs

Smartphones become of interest for surveillance and espionage purposes in direct proportion to their incidence – as mentioned at the beginning of this book, almost one and a half billion devices were sold worldwide in 2016. It is not just a matter of them being used as active espionage tools but of spying on the smartphone user themselves.

Individual persons can be purposefully monitored; their e-mail communication, SMS or instant messaging can be intercepted; and their current location constantly reported. This is meanwhile possible without much ado with a highly personal device such as a smartphone and suitable software. The device's technical specifications, which make it a small computer with Internet access, and above all the usage habits of users, who carry their phones with them almost everywhere, help here.

For years, there has been a grey market for commercial products which make smartphone surveillance accessible to anyone who is prepared to invest a few euros. Apart from a basic technical understanding in handling software and a PayPal account or credit card, all that is needed is brief, unobserved access to the device itself to install the appropriate software.

I tried this myself for a contribution to television programme *Akte 20.13* on channel Sat1. In this case, the "victim" of the surveillance was, of course, informed in advance about the whole thing.

A provider of such software has the following to say about possible applications:

> Do you suspect that your child is taking drugs or meeting the wrong kind of people? Or would you like to know whether your employees are working while you are not in the office? What chatrooms do your children visit, and above all, with whom? Certainty is everything! No monthly costs and no subscription – you pay just once for the desired validity period.

Other providers in Great Britain or the United States refer to multilanguage support hotlines, offer a money-back guarantee or even compete against each other for market leadership or about the question of who actually invented the original spy software for smartphones. The US FlexiSPY company claims to have been the inventor of the segment in 2004 and to still be the current technological leader today. Their competitor, mSpy, on the other hand, goes for being well known on radio and TV, refers to numerous media reports on their product and claims to have a million customers worldwide. Whether and to what extent the figures from this shady sector can be believed is quite another matter.

However, there is something else here which is interesting. The advertising regularly uses the same arguments and then always refers to more or less the same scenarios: protecting children, monitoring possibly unfaithful spouses and partners and surveilling employees. Evil be to he who evil thinks, but at least all the products I tested remind you that the permission of those being monitored must always be sought before the software is installed or put into operation. The alleged testimonial of a certain "Anthony Gassmann, director" which mSpy used in its advertising was really pleasant:

> Managing a large company is not as easy as you might think – you should always keep an eye on your staff so that they don't publish confidential company data. mSpy was the perfect choice for me to stay on the ball.

Although this statement is no longer available on the mSpy website, the basic feature set remains the same as well as all the use cases one can think of. Such tools are in fact suitable not only for the surveillance of employees, which is illegal in many countries, but also for spying on the competition. As already indicated, just brief access to the target person's mobile device is enough to install the software for permanent surveillance.

So much for the theory or the marketing promises of the providers. However, all of the products I tested exhibit weaknesses. The selected surveillance results do not arrive in anything near real time as suggested by the providers but sometimes only after a considerable delay. The side effects of installation are, however, critical as they increase the risk of discovery. The current software does hide itself so well that it can't be found by someone who doesn't know where to look, and it takes up very little storage space. However, it causes an increase in data transmission volume and noticeably higher battery usage. An enlightened user could notice that something is wrong with their smartphone.

In fact, the only case I have so far encountered in the wild is one of the director in the construction industry who noticed the much shorter battery life of his mobile phone following a personal meeting with consortium partners as part of a larger construction project. An external company commissioned by the IT department finally discovered the spy software. Whoever had slipped it on to his phone was never discovered, but the threat was detected and eliminated by replacing the phone with a brand new one. Even if this case passed off without damage, the number of cases which go unreported must be huge if the easy accessibility and handling of these solutions for "domestic espionage" are taken as a benchmark.

Shockingly, there are offers for problem-free espionage by anyone. An IT company in Milan with the telling name of Hacking Team promises all-round surveillance of smartphones in the documentation for its Galileo Remote Control System product – although admittedly for the purposes of surveillance by the authorities. The function list is huge. A detailed analysis of the system by the Citizen Lab at the University of Toronto lists the software's options for access to the victim's smartphone (Citizenlab 2014): address book, applications used and file accesses, calendar, contacts, stored passwords, call data and recordings of conversations, screenshots, photos from the built-in camera, access to the phone's microphone, the phone location, Internet sites visited, bugging of phone conversations and setup and automatic activation of a conference call with the person doing the surveillance as the third, unnoticed participant. In short, it offers comprehensive surveillance of the users which goes far beyond the possibilities of already-familiar commercial tools. What is particularly remarkable about this solution is also that it goes easy on the battery capacity and transmission volume and is therefore much harder to discover. It is thus possible to transmit data only in particular constellations, for example when logging on to a wireless LAN or connecting to a charger.

The handbook "RCS9: The Hacking Suite for Governmental Interception", given by Hacking Team to their customers, from which Citizen Lab also quotes extracts, exhibits sophisticated installation methods which go far beyond that quoted previously and only partly require direct access to the phone in addition to a complex infrastructure which is intended to help disguise the surveillant even if the software is discovered on the device. The malware can thus be smuggled in in collaboration with the network operator or attached to downloads as an unwanted addition. It almost seems to go without saying that the software can be updated and if necessary uninstalled again remotely. Precisely this company's PC software also brings a similar range of functions: there is then practically nothing to stand in the way of the all-round surveillance of a single target person.

Even if this software – as the mobile phone forensics software mentioned previously – is officially only available to state institutions as part of "lawful interception" – in other words eavesdropping on a legal basis – and the provider expressly points out that it does not supply states which could commit violations of human rights and also not private organisations, we must still assume that precisely such software can and probably already has fallen into the hands of criminals. What is commercially available on the grey market is just a foretaste of what – assuming sufficient financial means – is also available for economically motivated espionage. Entrepreneurs and security officers are well advised to assume that surveillance services and espionage programmes which are available to state bodies are also accessible for private companies and therefore curious competitors.

Google Glass

A great deal has already been written about the smart glasses which Google brought to market under the name of Google Glass. This is a technical device which looks like a pair of spectacles but in no way corrects your eyesight. Instead, it has a small display and a small number of functions which help the wearer to take photos or film short videos more or less unobtrusively. The further fields of application, such as picture recognition functions or identifying people, are interesting. Someone who has a bad memory for faces would thus be able to read off the name and other helpful information. From a technical point of view, Google Glass is nothing less than a small computer consisting of a central processor and RAM, a touch operation field with a trigger button, a microphone, a digital camera for photos and videos, a loudspeaker, Bluetooth and wireless LAN antennae, an acceleration sensor with a gyroscope and a rechargeable battery. In addition to these integrated controls, Google also even permits individual functions to be triggered by blinking.

Enthusiasm for the product at Google itself was huge, at least initially: the manager responsible for the product at Google is even quoted as saying, "the ability to outsource our brain to a device like this will just make us so much better" (Google 2014). There was some resistance to this much hubris even in Silicon Valley: smart-glasses wearers were berated as "glassholes" or even attacked personally. Some restaurants, casinos, bars and even public institutions issued bans.

From a data protection perspective, what is relevant is the coupling of Google Glass with the services of the Internet giant Google Services. This means that all information recorded is inevitably channelled via Google's servers. This causes fundamental doubts that Google Glass is at all suitable for use in a working environment, for example in manufacturing industry. In some cases it can certainly make sense to reflect the necessary steps for assembling or repairing a device into a manufacturing employee's or machine technician's field of vision via smart glasses so that he or she has both hands free for his or her work. In many areas, however, the associated passing on of work instructions and content from the user's field of view and hearing to Google – and thus possibly to the NSA and especially private contractors of the NSA – can hardly be acceptable. For even if we believe the claims of the American government that their Secret Service is not involved in industrial espionage activities and its sole interest is in combatting terror, it cannot be ruled out that employees of private companies associated with the NSA may access the stored data and pass it on to friendly companies. The revelations by Edward Snowden – an employee of a private service provider working for the NSA – especially have shown to what extent data drains are possible.

But Google Glass is not only a security risk for this reason. The smart glasses can also help to spy on the password and system access of third parties. This is really obvious and requires little explanation; some readers may even object that normally "looking closely" is enough in order to spy out an access code for a tablet or smartphone. This is indeed correct, but this possibility is further extended through the suitable use of Google Glass or similar camera technology. Researchers at Lowell University in Massachusetts have, for example, developed software which analyses the shadows cast by the fingers which occur when typing in passwords and inferred the password from this. A direct line of sight to the device or to the display of the smartphone or tablet is thus no longer necessary. The consequences are dramatic, and besides a complete ban for Google Glass and similar devices in the company, employees must be sensitised to the fact that devices used in public places in this way can be spied on.

The problem will become even more acute with further wearables – devices which can be worn on the body like glasses, a watch or a piece of clothing or jewellery. It is foreseeable that the upcoming smartwatch boom will bring with it a whole load of video components which will be even more suitable for spying as well as being much less conspicuous to use than Google Glass.

On the subject of Google Glass, Google in 2014 announced a collaboration with the globally leading spectacles manufacturer Luxottica and wants to bring out models together under the Ray-Ban and Oakley brands. "We can expect these to be much less conspicuous than the first generation and that in further product cycles the implementation of a display and a camera in the glasses will constantly become less visible" (Luxottica 2014). In other words, the wearable spy camera is back in a new guise – and even more dangerous than before.

Even if the media interest on Google Glass has declined and there have been no follow-ups to the 2014 announcement to date, there are other iterations of the same idea about to enter the market. Think Spectacles by Snap, which are currently only sunglasses that can record short bits of video to transmit via Snapchat but may bring more acceptance of video-oriented wearables to the society. And just recently – in 2017 – Google Glass resurfaced. The new Google Glass "enterprise edition" is available to corporate customers only (Wired 2017). Time will tell whether we see some additional versions anywhere soon.

Built-in risks

A back door which is secured either inadequately or not at all is every attacker's dream. Such back doors in technical systems are constantly becoming known and are consequently purposefully attacked or are even being created in the first place by attackers – in preparation for further attacks.

Open back doors

Real-life burglars often get in through the back door because it is usually less well secured than the main entrance, or is sometimes even open. In the field of IT, the term "back door" also stands for an area which is only inadequately secured or even not secured at all against intruders from outside. These are undocumented official entrances which permit access to stored data. These back doors play an important role in many successful attack attempts on IT systems for the purpose of spying. However, the general public rarely hears anything about them. Such back doors are continually being discovered, mainly by chance.

The French security specialist Eloi Vanderbeken was thus able to document a security vulnerability which occurred in an identical form in several router models from various manufacturers (Github 2014). This was suitable for gaining control over the router, reading out the administrator password or resetting the router to the factory settings – and thus possibly temporarily disabling the Internet connection for a private household or small company which uses the router. As a result, at least one of the manufacturers affected offered a free software update. Cisco – one of the companies in question – described the security vulnerability as an undocumented test interface which could be exploited by an attacker to gain control over the router (Cisco 2014).

The big question is, why were several manufacturers equally affected? The answer was as simple as it was shocking: because all of them work with the same components. In this case, the problem was traced to a DSL modem from the

Taiwanese manufacturer Sercomm which Cisco, Netgear, Diamond and LevelOne as well as possibly other manufacturers had integrated into their routers – obviously without adequately testing it. It was by all means conceivable that the developers at Sercomm had actually only built in the back door for testing purposes and then forgotten to remove the relevant function again in the finished product.

Unfortunately, it must be principally assumed that such a negligent business practise is no isolated incident but a common thing in the technology sector. IT company representatives may get het up about this, but comparing the arrangements for tests in information technology and test arrangements in the automotive industry makes it clear that something has to be wrong. It is therefore no wonder that apart from the router in question a number of other cases exist which affect a wide variety of devices.

At the Black Hat hacker conference in 2013, the security expert Craig Heffner pointed out that there are back doors hidden in a number of webcams in the form of permanently programmed administrator passwords which permit attackers to film unnoticed or even to manipulate the firmware via the Internet in certain webcam models from D-Link, Trendnet or IQinVision. It was especially striking that not only cheap webcams from DIY stores were affected but also cameras used for surveillance purposes in companies. In his research paper (Heffner 2013), published for the conference, Heffner explained that due to this security vulnerability an attacker could not only look at the camera's video stream but also manipulate it. A still picture could, for example, be "frozen" so that intruders could gain access to company premises or an especially secured area unnoticed by security. Those who are reminded of thrillers or spy films like *Mission Impossible* or *Ocean's 11* are absolutely right. The potential available to a creative attack team can be enormous in some cases.

Hardware and software manufacturers always use the argument that back doors are useful, for example, to reset a device remotely when a customer has locked themselves out with a faulty configuration. Too bad if this comes to light by chance and thus perhaps helps attackers to gain control of a device. That this can sometimes even be quite trivial is shown by the case of two Canadian schoolchildren who allegedly brought an ATM under their control by means of the handbook for the machine which they had found by chance on the Internet and a password which they were able to guess at their first attempt. Whoever had previously assumed that such sensitive areas such as cash supply are specially protected now knows better after this example. Fortunately, the two boys contacted the bank and did not succumb to the temptation to make money out of the security vulnerability they had found.

The Japanese network equipment specialist Allied Telesis also spectacularly attracted attention in 2011 with a built-in back door. According to reports by specialist media (Heise 2011), they had accidentally placed information on the back doors to their own products in the website's support area. Amongst other things, there was a description of how to give back access to a user who was locked out by means of a standard password. The corresponding password lists and serial numbers of the devices were available for download. The industry service *Heise* quoted the website, which is of course no longer available, with the words (Heise 2011):

> The back door passwords listed here are only intended for internal use. Do not make this information freely available to the customer as they are suitable for compromising a network. Request the MAC address and serial number of the device and also proof of purchase from the customer if he requires a back door password. This ensures that the user is actually authorised to access the device.

This instruction made it clear that the information was not intended for the public under any circumstances. According to a report published by *Heise* not long after, the manufacturer regarded this not as a problem but a "normal function in the industry" (Heise 2011).

A whole other set of technical devices are plagued not by "normal functions" but simple errors. As early as in 2014, a vulnerability was discovered in millions of televisions which can be used to control the television. Of course, initially this caused some amusement and conjured up amusing scenes: an angry attacker switches over to a romantic movie in the middle of the football world championship. However, the laughter may well stick in your throat if you assume that such televisions also have integrated video cameras for Skype and other services and stand in numerous conference rooms. The inconspicuous remote-controlled switching on of the audio and video transmission to the outside would be the perfect surveillance setup – directly in the heart of the target company. The security researchers Yossi Oren and Angelos Keromytis, who discovered and documented this vulnerability, also point out on their website that it is possible to attack other systems attached to the Internet via just such a hijacked television (Keromytis 2014).

That is indeed possible to use a smart television as a bug to listen to the conversations of people in the same room, at least with some device types. This was brought to light by the WikiLeaks "Vault7" publications, which were mentioned earlier in this book, although it is not clear whether there was a back door or programming error as the basis for this attack.

A back door is not always left in by the manufacturer deliberately or through negligence. Sometimes third parties are involved, as one of Edward Snowden's many revelations about the NSA has shown. The journalist Glenn Greenwald wrote about a special approach in his book, later covered by the newspaper the *Guardian* (Greenwald 2014): the NSA can intercept servers and other computer network devices before they are delivered to the customer, then take their time implanting back doors for monitoring users, repackage the devices including the factory seal and then send them on. The NSA thus gains access to entire network infrastructures and their users. Greenwald also wrote that there is no proof that the manufacturers affected knew about this. It must be borne in mind that such methods for implementing back doors are not only available to the NSA or other intelligence services but under certain circumstances also to competitors who can gain access to the logistics chain: the corrupt employee of a supplier can be the gateway in.

Companies that want to be absolutely certain therefore use services which guarantee the integrity of the equipment ordered with suitable tests. Phones are, for example, X-rayed and checked for manipulation of the hardware and only installed after tests have been carried out. Fink Secure Communication, which is based near Coburg in the Franconia region of Germany, specialises in such examinations and has developed its own X-ray machines which uncover manipulations. However, if an attacker succeeds in installing modified software without being noticed, this is usually difficult to spot.

The problems in connection with supervisory control and data acquisition (SCADA) systems really are deserving of a mention. In the market for industrial control systems, known internationally as SCADA, which is dominated by Siemens, there are sometimes passwords which are fixed and the same everywhere (Wired 2010b). In this case, the problem was caused by technical developments: such control systems, some of which have been in operation for 20 years or more, were not intended to be operated in a networked environment – they were to run constantly in an enclosed network environment or as individual systems.

The increasing networking of our world now brings new problems fur such control systems – not so much as regards industrial espionage but rather sabotage. Joe Weiss, the author of the book titled *Protecting Industrial Control Systems from Electronic Threats*, reports that industrial control systems were primarily developed with the focus on efficiency and that IT security was generally not a particular requirement. He assumes that around half of providers of industrial control systems use such hard-wired passwords in their systems (Weiss 2010). Knowing that power station operators and public utility companies have such systems in use could make you very nervous.

Incidents like that in Dallas, where all emergency sirens went off at once one Friday night in 2017 since being hacked, do not help build trust to connected machinery and devices.

But how can security vulnerabilities and configuration errors be found? It would be possible to write a script, a programme which queries hundreds of thousands of IP addresses and reports possible finds. This is a laborious undertaking and not easy for the layman to accomplish. How convenient that there is a search machine just for this: the search page for security gaps in the Internet is called Shodan. Back doors, configuration errors and other system vulnerabilities of devices connected to the Internet such as webcams, industrial controls and other devices can be found here. This search engine is known as the "Google for hackers" in IT security circles.

Like other search engines, Shodan trawls through the Internet and stores the results collected in a database. Any user can now trawl through Shodan: for example, for the search term "default password", this special search machine lists systems accessible via the Internet in which it is possible to log in via standard gateways together with further useful information. Every system administrator can profit from this information to close security gaps, but equally attackers can also use it to prepare an attack.

It is possible to find information online on all kinds of devices with weaknesses, for example webcams, with the assistance of corresponding search terms or a combination of them. If you look more closely, you will discover that in the United Kingdom alone, hundreds of thousands of webcams can be hijacked via documented security vulnerabilities. A simple comparison of the IP address ranges with the known Internet address ranges of certain companies easily supplies the correct intersecting set for a targeted attack.

Although of course webcams are not the only target of attack. In a research paper titled "Searching Shodan for Fun and Profit", the security researcher Sajal Verma listed which devices can actually be found with Shodan (Verma 2014): servers, routers, network switches, printers with public IP addresses, webcams, VoIP phones and SCADA systems. In this document, Verma also supplies an instruction manual for Shodan and describes how to combine the search machine with other system security tools via a programming interface made available by the provider to perform queries automatically. What is dangerous about this is that Shodan makes it possible for anyone to search for security vulnerabilities and prepare for their use. Some elementary knowledge and a small financial budget are enough, as use of the search machine is subject to a fee beyond certain test functions.

But Shodan is not the problem by itself. It is the so-called Internet of Things (IoT) where more and more everyday devices – from lightbulbs to dishwashers – are getting connected to the net without taking the necessary steps to secure them. There are hundreds of examples of insecure IoT devices out there. To stick with lightbulbs and dishwashers, in 2014 security company Contextis found out that smart lightbulbs by LIFX could be attacked successfully to gain access to the Wi-Fi security credentials as a foundation for further spying on the target company (Contextis 2014). And just recently researchers found security holes in Miele professional dishwashers used in canteens which could be possibly used for further attacks on corporate networks (The Register 2017b).

Funnily enough, just a few weeks later Miele published an advertisement of a vacancy for an "Expert IoT Security" on their website. Unlike a compromised webcam, a compromised dishwasher probably can't be used to spy on you, at least not directly. But every device owned by an outsider can be the foundation to attack further devices and computer systems within your network, so any insecurity in any device in your network should be taken care of.

There is no easy way to secure individual devices, especially if most manufacturers – other than the two mentioned previously that issued firmware fixes to the problems – do not care about updates once the devices are shipped. It is highly recommended to provide network segments separated from the rest of your corporate infrastructure for IoT devices and industrial control systems.

The problem that surfaces here is the core problem of the information age. IT companies have found a way to avoid liability for the products they ship – or at least found a way to get away with it, unlike the aircraft or automotive industry. In consequence, software products and products with software embedded, like all the IoT devices mentioned previously, are typically prone to errors. "Ship fast and fix later" seems to be the motto of most suppliers. This motto is echoed in Silicon Valley culture; just think about Facebook's mission statement which is or at least contained the phrase "move fast and break things".

While making software companies liable for their product is unlikely and there might not be a simple solution in sight, there already is an easy fix – with unwanted side effects: the BrickerBot. BrickerBot is a malware that was found in the wild by cybersecurity firm Radware in early 2017. BrickerBot attacks IoT devices and intentionally bricks them by corrupting their storage capability and reconfiguring kernel parameters. The result is an IoT device that is rendered useless within seconds after getting infected. To bring these devices back to life, the owner will need to update them. To date, BrickerBot only attacks certain devices built on a special software stack.

It is possible that similar attacks in the future can be used to sabotage factories by attacking certain SCADA systems or corporate headquarters by attacking facility management control systems – think elevators, lighting, climate control systems, you name it.

The attack of the hand scanner

The hand scanners used by logistics companies and in warehouse environments which help to record and trace shipments are familiar to all of us. The best-known example of use is the recording of parcels by logistics service providers. Whether UPS, DHL, GLS, DPD or Hermes, anyone who has ever ordered something in an online shop is familiar with these devices and their characteristic bleep when the courier scans the barcode and the recipient has to scratch some kind of signature on a display using something akin to a plastic scraper to confirm receipt of the package.

These hand scanners are used not only by couriers out on the road but also in warehouses to document the arrival and departure of goods simply and without errors.

Frequent travellers may also be familiar with the devices at large car rental stations where a returned vehicle is treated in exactly the same way as a parcel being delivered – a quick scan of the barcode, a brief visual inspection of the vehicle and finished.

What not many know is that the hand scanners which are used for all these different purposes all come from Chinese manufacturers and use some form of embedded operating system as the basis for the logistics software which is normally provided by the relevant company. In 2014, the American TrapX cybersecurity company succeeded in proving that such scanners had been used to perform targeted espionage attacks on financial data stored in companies (TrapX 2014). In this case, a certain provider's hand scanners were infected with malware. This malware attempted to detect servers with financial data in the company network and to install a Trojan on them which allowed remote access. To do this, the malware overcame internal firewalls which were supposed to separate the wireless network in which the scanners were operated from the remaining company network. Other security measures, such as the certificate-controlled logging in of devices, also offered no adequate protection in this particular case because the scanners used were apparently already infected with the malware on leaving the manufacturer. On top of this, the provider's support website also contained the same software: a system update would therefore have restored the initial situation, including the malware. It was not possible to uncover who was behind this, but TrapX's investigations indicated that it could possibly be attributed to the Lanxiang Vocational School, familiar to security experts from other attacks, which in turn is closely associated with the Chinese People's Liberation Army.

In this case the devices used the Windows Embedded operating system. Less well known than the almost omnipresent variants on computers and notebooks, Windows Embedded was a modular version of Windows especially adapted to the needs of device manufacturers. Its successor is now called Windows IoT. Such embedded systems also run mainly invisibly in many other places, on Blu-ray players, set-top boxes, washing machines, medical technical equipment or aviation equipment.

You could almost conjure up a little sympathy for a security expert who was interviewed by *SecurityWeek* magazine about an actual case (Securityweek 2014): all equipment brought into the company should be thoroughly tested in order to detect "hostile activities" at an early stage and isolate them – before this equipment is used in a production environment. That doesn't really seem to be a realistic alternative considering that any such test would probably cost a lot more than the purchase price. It makes more sense not to order the cheapest equipment but to buy it from an established provider with long-term experience. This doesn't guarantee absolute security either, but it does significantly reduce the probability of becoming the victim of an attack. Separating environments in which such systems are used from critical parts of the company as far as possible would certainly also help.

Such attacks represent a new risk potential if the criticality of malware supplied with equipment is compared to the exploitation of existing security vulnerabilities. As a reminder, a case recently made the headlines in which the G Data security company discovered more or less permanently installed malware on new mobile phones from a Chinese manufacturer which permitted the user to be spied on remotely, which included accessing all stored data, eavesdropping on conversations and remotely activating the phone's microphone.

Unlike in the example of the hand scanners, the purpose in this case is not quite clear. It is unlikely that companies were to be spied on in this way as they rarely buy cheap, no-name smartphones.

However, this development is still worrying. It doesn't take a prophet to see that technical equipment of all kinds with built-in malware used in companies will probably be one of the biggest security nightmares of the near future. This is even more so considering the fact that because of the Internet of Things and Industry 4.0, which both require the networking of non-PCs, we can expect a lot more of these types of devices, including the associated security risks.

New security hazards

New opportunities breed new hazards. This has been shown in several cases in this book already. But sometimes it is simply quality improvements of technologies which have been available for years that change the rule of the game. Sometimes it is just the mix between social engineering skills and technological advancements.

We need to get into more details here so we can understand the motives of the attackers.

Aspects of quality and quantity

It is not only new technologies and end devices which can be used for espionage; often, misuse is only possible because of quality improvements or a new form of information acquisition. Take smartphone cameras with high-resolution screens, for example, which take outstanding photos without flash even in unfavourable lighting conditions – stealing information occasionally is no longer a problem. The performance of high-quality smartphones today is sufficient to record the content of all screens in an airport lounge or a coffee house. As mentioned earlier, even reflections in spectacle lenses or eyes can be enough.

Classical espionage tools such as bugs or minicameras have made considerable progress in recent years: on the one hand, usable devices have become smaller and therefore easier to hide, and on the other, the picture resolution and microphone sensitivity of top devices have improved significantly. At the same time, there have been developments such as passive elements which are extremely hard to discover because they are not given away by emissions.

Increasing Internet bandwidths and the comprehensive availability of fast mobile communication connections also contribute to making it easier for attackers to grab information whilst simultaneously reducing the risk of being discovered. Syphoning off large quantities of data would have been noticed just a few years ago because of the sudden increase in data volume or a deteriorating network connection. Today, it can be assumed that even considerable data flows often remain undiscovered simply because they get lost in the background noise – in other words as part of normal transmission quantities.

Storage media with which data can be physically drawn from a computer have become consistently cheaper in recent years. At the same time, the maximum storage volume has grown along with the transfer rate. High-capacity USB sticks and SD cards with 64, 128 or 256 gigabytes of storage capacity are now available at online retailers as well as in supermarkets for very little money and are ideally suited for collecting and drawing off huge quantities of intellectual capital in companies – just brief access is enough.

How great the danger of information being drained due to data carriers can be seen from the numerous cases of CDs or DVDs with customer data from Swiss banks which have naturally aroused great interest amongst tax authorities of other countries like the United States and Germany.

The same goes with the so-called Panama Papers. In 2015 more than 11.5 million documents were leaked by an anonymous source. The Panama Papers contained information for more than 200,000 offshore entities and belonged to the Panamanian law firm Mossack Fonseca, which acted as a corporate service provider for wealthy individuals and public officials throughout the world to hide their assets.

Both cases may not involve spying on the competition, but they work in exactly the same way in the context of industrial espionage: a few years ago, an employee had little chance of taking more than a few individual customer records or maybe a copy of a file. Comprehensive digitalisation and the simultaneous increase in storage volume and reduction in storage media costs make it possible today to steal and pass on thousands of customer profiles en masse. This development increases the risk potential from industrial and economic espionage tremendously.

Social engineering as a risk factor

DEF CON is one of the largest hacker conferences worldwide. It is held yearly in Las Vegas, Nevada. There, the interested visitor learns a great deal about security questions and can buy corresponding equipment from software tools to tools for opening door locks; regular hacker competitions are also staged.

DEF CON 21 was especially remarkable. DEF CON 21 took place at the beginning of August 2013 in Las Vegas – with 15,000 participants from all over the world. This time, one aim of that year's capture-the-flag competition was to obtain business-critical information via personal contact. Ten companies from the Fortune 500 list of the largest companies were chosen as targets. The result: for the participants in the competition, all "techies", who are not regarded as having particularly high social competence, it was really simple to find out sensitive business information by means of a simple phone call by, for example, posing as a student, supplier or colleague of the person on the other end of the phone. In this way, information about systems deployed and their details, wireless LAN networks or building safety got into the wrong hands.

From the point of view of the attackers, the comprehensive profiles and activities of target company employees on Facebook, LinkedIn, Twitter and other social networks are especially helpful. Many interesting pieces of information were obtained in advance through targeted analysis of the relevant social media sources. In addition, the information gathered there helped to find the right way in to the phone conversation; after all, a lot of background information on the person being phoned had been gathered. In a large number of cases this meant that a certain familiarity occurred which the attacker was able to exploit. What was tried out here as a game is one of the main methods of obtaining information and is known as social engineering.

For cyberspies, who are after company secrets and information on new products, company takeovers or market developments, it is much easier to reach for the phone and simply call rather than spend lots of time preparing and performing a targeted attack with specially written malware. But of course, it would be just as possible to tailor malware on the basis of information on system security gained from a personal conversation. In such cases, social engineering just serves as a way in for a larger attack.

Thus, social engineering is when attackers use normal human reactions to gain access to information which is valuable to them. Initial starting points for social engineering attacks are usually apparently "unimportant" employees but also service providers and suppliers. The attacker works themselves forwards through these. Professional attackers exploit perfectly normal human characteristics such as helpfulness, obedience to authority, craving for recognition, insecurity, laziness, fear of confrontation or need for harmony.

Inexperienced "victims" normally either don't notice these communicative techniques at all or much too late, which is why most internal company compliance regulations are of little help. Legally speaking, such methods are difficult to impossible to apprehend.

Whilst personal contact is always at the centre of social engineering attacks, technology is by all means also used in this context. An employee who is not specially trained will always assume that the number of the caller visible on the display is always the correct one and therefore assume that it is a colleague calling – whilst in reality an attacker wishes to create this impression with a false caller ID in order to build up a personal attack on this basis. Training for employees which makes clear how easy such features can be faked therefore appears to be urgently necessary.

Attacks via Facebook and other social media

The kinds of dangers which can emanate from social media were formidably demonstrated by security researcher Thomas Ryan in 2010. During an experiment over a period of 28 days, which he subsequently reported on at the Black Hat conference, he invented a fictional person who only existed in the social networks of Facebook, Twitter and LinkedIn.

His report, which was aptly titled "Getting into Bed with Robin Sage", revealed numerous details (Ryan 2010): a young lady named Robin Sage with an attractive profile photo allegedly worked for the US Navy as an analyst for cybersecurity and was allegedly a graduate of the elite Massachusetts Institute of Technology (MIT). Within just one month, Ryan succeeded in collecting 300 high-ranking contacts in the military and industry with his fictional persona Robin Sage – and in obtaining confidential information on the US military from them. Amongst other things, Robin Sage received job offers from Google and the arms manufacturer Lockheed Martin as well as invitations to dinner.

The new contacts were mainly men, which was perhaps no great surprise: Ryan had taken the profile photo he used from a pornography website.

Ryan had also left numerous clues which should have made military security experts suspicious: the name of the fictitious person was the same as that of an exercise by elite US troops, and the address stated was the address of the military service provider Blackwater (Dark 2010). Nevertheless, hardly any of the high-ranking military people and security experts became sceptical. Even people who allegedly worked in the same building accepted Ryan's contact requests. However, if even high-ranking military security experts fall for such tricks, how can you expect a normal employee in a company to treat approach attempts carefully?

An especially fruitful place for such fake contacts seems to be the LinkedIn business network. I have also frequently been contacted by people who had a seemingly plausible profile with extensive sector contacts but turned out not to be genuine. Fending off such fakes is, however, relatively easy: do not confirm any contact request from a person who you do not know personally.

That the case of Robin Sage is no theoretical construction became clear at the beginning of 2014 as the security consulting company iSight from Dallas uncovered a similar approach by Iranian hackers (Reuters 2014a). Apparently, high-ranking military personnel, embassy employees and other officials were amongst the victims. The hackers' aim was to obtain access data for government and company networks and also information on weapons systems and diplomatic negotiations. The attackers claimed to be employees of a fictitious news website or from companies which worked for the military and other organisations. For this, they created fake profiles on Facebook, LinkedIn, Google+ and Twitter, including appropriate fictitious personal content. The hackers did not address their targets directly but built up contacts to their relatives, friends and colleagues and thus created a basis for trust. Contacts to more than 2,000 persons were created in this way by the 14 faked identities.

Even after this indirect making of contact, the hacker initially acted with great care and continued to work at building up mutual trust by sending interesting news articles which of course were not infected with malware. Only later, in the course of the carefully built up contacts, was any attempt made to plant links which led to sites which were infested with malware or directly to fake web portals where victims were tricked into entering their access data.

Economic espionage and sabotage

When talking to company security officers, it quickly becomes clear that the fear of sabotage by third parties is almost as widespread as the perception of the hazard of industrial espionage, especially in production companies. Security vulnerabilities in so-called SCADA systems and computerised control units for machines were perceived as especially worrying – after all, a machine controlled in this way normally cannot be completely separated from the network. Meanwhile, there are security providers, such as the German Genua company, which specialise in security measures in production facilities and which – working on the assumption that all systems are inherently insecure – provide security equipment which only temporarily permits necessary maintenance access and otherwise completely seals off the machine control.

The risk of sabotage is, however, not limited to large companies and production facilities. The manipulation of Internet services with the intention of damaging competitors is simple but effective. At the latest, since companies have recognised the significance of online evaluations for the consumer decisions of end customers, astounding effects can be observed in several sectors, above all in the tourism industry: one's own offering is praised in the highest tones and that of the competition put down. This is certainly not sabotage in the normal sense, but it points the way to new, perfidious methods which can ultimately be a threat to a company's existence.

Companies in the offline world become dependent on the information online being correct to the extent that users rely on online services. According to a report in *Wired* magazine, a restaurant in Washington had to close down after guests stayed away: somebody had manipulated the data in Google Maps and simply removed the opening times of the restaurant at the weekend which are vital for its continued existence. The landlord, who was in his mid-70s and was certainly not terribly talented online, was quickly surprised about the particularly noticeable 75 percent reduction in guests, but he was only informed very late about the sabotage – too late for his restaurant (Poulsen 2014).

Basically, such manipulations are only possible because, like other services, Google Maps relies solely on crowdsourcing, where frauds have an easy time with data acquisition. In a test, a creative hacker even succeeded in creating new branches of the FBI and the US Secret Service with phone numbers and got these listed on Google Maps. He also rerouted calls to these numbers to the correct addresses and was able to listen in at the same time – not sabotage, but an interesting form of espionage attack (Tiku 2014).

In principle, Google Maps, Yelp and the rest are a modern substitute for the Yellow Pages and other printed industry directories. The information in them is trusted, at least as regards to locations, phone numbers and opening times. Users also extend this trust to the digital world. The result is a practically ideal starting point for malicious manipulation in terms of sabotage and espionage.

Industrial espionage and cybercrime

It is impossible to contemplate modern methods of spying on companies by using information and communications technologies without reference to the big picture. The term widely used here is "cybercrime".

The US National Center for Crime Prevention (ncpc.org) defines "cybercrime" as follows (NCPC 2012):

> A crime committed or facilitated via the Internet is a cybercrime. Cybercrime is any criminal activity involving computers and networks. It can range from fraud to unsolicited emails (spam). It can include the distant theft of government or corporate secrets through criminal trespass into remote systems

around the globe. Cybercrime incorporates anything from downloading illegal music files to stealing millions of dollars from online bank accounts. Cybercrime also includes non-money offenses, such as creating viruses on other computers or posting confidential business information on the Internet.

Of course, this is a really broad definition. Similar definitions of the term can be found in other countries.

In its annual crime statistics report, the German Federal Office of Criminal Investigation (BKA) defines cybercrime as "all crimes which are committed either using modern information and communications technology or against it" (BKA 2012). The BKA classifies the spying on and interception of data together with data modification, computer sabotage and fraud with access authorisations, computer fraud and forging evidentiary data as cybercrime. In its report on the current situation for 2012, the BKA itself states:

> It is not possible to assess the phenomenon of cybercrime purely on the basis of statistics. Individual and especially relevant phenomena such as phishing in the area of online banking, blackmail in connection with DDoS attacks or the many other manifestations of digital extortion (e.g. ransomware) are not recorded under cybercrime in police crime statistics but rather under police codes for individual offences.

What is emerging here is a very distinct demarcation problem in terms of fighting crime which is not easy to solve. The BKA is of course not alone in this – this topic is being discussed by specialists all around the globe. At the Cybercrime in the World Today Conference at Pace University in Manhattan in 2013, the New York district attorney spoke of the topic of cybercrime as the fastest growing form of crime in the city and declared that almost every crime now involved cybercrime (Epoch 2013).

The European Agency for Network and Information Security (ENISA) has produced a current investigation into cybercrime. As part of a metastudy, 50 reports by IT security companies, authorities and computer emergency response teams (CERT) from the first half of 2013 were analysed and the following conclusions drawn (VDI 2013): criminals increasingly use anonymization technologies and peer-to-peer systems to prevent their attacks from being discovered and undone, and turn to mobile technologies more and more often. The combination of malware, hacking tools, anonymous payment methods and digital currencies such as Bitcoin offers new possibilities for fraud. Cyberattacks represented a major reason for the failure of telecommunications infrastructures. Attack scenarios were becoming ever-more sophisticated: attackers were meanwhile also using cloud services to launch their attacks. According to the report, the major threats are:

- Drive-by exploits in which a computer is infected in passing. Weaknesses in the browser, browser plug-ins and in the operating system are exploited to install malware unnoticed.

- Code injections. This is the addition of harmful codes to editable websites such as visitors' books or forums, which are used especially often against widely used content management (CMS) systems such as Joomla or WordPress.

Furthermore, the report also named the following threats: targeted attacks and identity theft as well as botnets, remotely controlled computer networks consisting of computers which communicate with one another and search engine poisoning, where users are enticed onto a page infected with malware with the help of manipulated search machine results. Whilst the prevalence of spam is decreasing, the incidence of phishing is unchanged. Compared to the previous years, there is a rising incidence of denial of service attacks and scareware, malware which intimidates users and is intended to get them to do certain things. In the last few years we have also seen a boom in what is called ransomware. Ransomware is a computer malware that installs covertly on a victim's computer and holds the victim's data hostage by automatically encrypting it with a key only known to the attacker. Subsequently, the software offers the victim to the opportunity to buy back his or her data by selling him or her the key, typically after a payment has been made in Bitcoins. Other variants of ransomware steal the data and threaten the victim with the publishing of confidential or private information if no ransom is paid within a certain time frame. These attacks are typically carried out by sending out e-mails with compromised attachments disguised as legitimate bills, Excel spread sheets or Word documents which – when opened – install the malware on the victim's computer.

Due to the large overlap with tools which are used in espionage attacks, it is worth keeping an eye on these general trends in cybercrime.

The methods used by cybercriminals have been well known for several years, but the extent of the damage they do is not clear. Very often publications in this field work with numbers which look like they were results of wild guesses or the extensive use of crystal balls. Most publications also miss to opportunity to correlate the numbers with key metrics of the economy.

A study which was published in 2014 by the IT security company McAfee and the Center for Strategic and International Studies (CSIS) in Washington managed that and gave an overview of the effects of cybercrime on the global economy: it alleged that between 0.5 and 0.8 percent of the world gross national product was lost annually due to cybercrime. Cybercrime therefore lies between maritime piracy (0.2 percent) and product knockoffs (0.9 percent) in significance. According to the authors of the study, many companies regarded this level of damage as acceptable: "Many companies expected shoplifting and take account of it in their pricing." However, the study also pointed out that it is practically impossible to provide precise figures. Most companies did not make such incidents public, partly because they are not aware of it and partly due to fear of negative publicity (WSJ 2014).

One gets an idea of how high this estimated number must be from Rudolf Proschko, head of counterintelligence for the Bavarian Regional Authority for the Protection of the Constitution, if he is to be believed: in the spring of 2013, he reported a large-scale attack on 102 Bavarian companies which took place in 2007. At the time, only two of them had noticed that strangers had broken into their company network (OVB 2013).

If you talk to company security officers about espionage activities by the competition, they frequently point out that they do not regard spying as the only threat. The perceived threat from sabotage to systems which could mean the interruption of operations is at least as great. Just imagine what damage a one-day stoppage of production at Volkswagen's main plant in Wolfsburg can cause. According to different sources, 3,800 vehicles a day were produced there in 2013. At an estimated average selling price of €20,000, the company would lose around €76 million in turnover should an attacker succeed in stopping production just for one day.

You may consider such attacks to be the stuff of wild speculation. But such attacks are by no means impossible, even if there are much easier targets. These are now examined in the next sections.

Your money or your network

The gambling industry has always been slightly dubious and subject to all kinds of legal regulation. It is intended to swell state coffers on the one hand and to protect the public from compulsive gambling on the other. The European national lotteries alone contribute more than €25 billion to national budgets. At least this is what the umbrella organisation of the national lotteries in Europe lists as official numbers on their website (European Lotteries 2017). And lotteries are just one part of the gambling industry. Think casinos and sports wagering.

The gambling industry is huge business and that makes it comprehensible that such potential also attracts entrepreneurs who want to test or exceed the limits of what is permissible.

The gambling industry was thus one of the first commercial sectors which was affected by digital changes. In the 1990s there were already online casinos which – mainly based in the Caribbean – attracted a global clientele and weren't bothered about national bans. The effects of the regulation of sports bets in several countries of mainland Europe were especially extreme. Unlike in UK sport, betting was and still is heavily regulated in most countries which leads to people seeking other ways to place their bets – ways that are sometimes illegal in the home country of the gambler.

One of the best-known sports bet providers online is Mybet.com. The company behind this is Personal Exchange International Ltd., which was founded in 2003, operates with a betting licence from Malta and quite naturally assumes that it can operate legally throughout the EU and in markets with special regulations for sports betting, like Germany (Mybet 2017):

> Yes, because mybet has various betting licences issued in the European Union. Due to the legally guaranteed European freedom of establishment and services these are fundamentally valid in all Member States of the EU.

The European Court of Justice reaffirmed its adjudication on this in September 2010 and declared the German monopoly on betting to be incompatible with European law. Against this background we presume that our services are also legal for the German market.

Whether this view would stand up in court has not yet been tested. But Mybet and other providers act inside a grey area which also attracts criminals.

Very soon after its founding, the company was the target of distributed denial of service (DDoS) attacks which were intended to paralyse the business with several simultaneous attacks on the online betting offices. The computer magazine *c't* reported a successful attack on Mybet lasting 16 hours: the company's website was not available during this time (Heise 2004). A provider like Mybet, which is exclusively online and generates turnover within a short time frame around a game event, is considerably weakened by such an attack. The attack was preceded by a blackmail attempt which Mybet had not taken seriously. According to media reports, at least two other online betting providers were affected by similar attacks in the same period. The attack was presumably performed by means of hijacked computers which were remote controlled in a botnet – which most computer users presumably do not notice.

What began at that time as a single attack and was mainly a problem with a grey area online has meanwhile become mainstream – just like suitable protection measures. Mybet sought help from DigiDefense, a company specialising in repelling such attacks – a service which Internet providers such as British Telecom, Deutsche Telekom or the Japanese NTT also provide today.

That such threats are no longer limited to criminals against criminals or criminals against the grey market is evident from other examples in which start-up companies, including the well-known provider Evernote, were the targets of DDoS attacks. Evernote provides a kind of to-do list application whose special feature is that it can automatically update tasks and notes across all of a user's devices. This central function was not available for several hours due to the attack (Inquirer 2014). The reason for this attack on Evernote was never discovered.

This example shows how at-risk companies which base their business model purely on the Internet are. A protection strategy including an emergency plan is urgently recommended for all companies which operate anything more than the obligatory "About Us" website online. This must take into account that such attacks can also serve to distract from the attackers' actual target – the theft of internal company data or customer data.

And the problem gets worse as more and more software applications and apps heavily rely on the availability of other services; sometimes several dozen services are necessary for just one smartphone app to work correctly. The good news is that more and more hosting companies as well as telecommunication providers offer affordable DDoS repelling services, a service that website owners should select and implement before it is too late.

Protection money 2.0

If the paralysing of a large Internet presence requires specialised technical knowledge, the new generation of online blackmailers normally travels light, as the following example shows. The operators of the 900 Degrees Neapolitan pizzeria in New Hampshire were astounded as they opened a letter which at first glance looked like junk mail but which turned out to be a genuine blackmailer's letter. In this printed, very individualised letter, the owner was informed that he was the target of blackmail. A kind of protection money payment was demanded in the form of the alternative online currency Bitcoin which permits anonymous payments.

To ensure the owner paid up, the following measures were threatened in the letter: complaints to the Better Business Bureau (the American equivalent of European consumer protection), the placement of fake orders, DDoS attacks on the reservation phone, bomb threats, vandalism and anonymous reports to the authorities of tax evasion or money laundering. According to investigations by various security experts, several restaurant operators received similar but individualised letters.

Blackmailing restaurant operators is of course nothing new. In 2010, the Italian newspaper *Il Sole 24 Ore* reported in detail on the problem in Italy and supplied data from a recently published study. According to this study, some 1.3 percent of Sicily's gross national product between 2002 and 2006 consisted of protection money payments – a profitable business with more than €1 billion per year in this region alone. Now it seems that technically competent criminals are trying to perfect extortion with 21st-century methods.

Industry 4.0 as a target for attack

A model known as Industry 4.0 which is receiving a great deal of attention among experts promises nothing less than "the next industrial revolution". The idea behind it is not only to network whole value-creation chains but also to achieve more or less autonomous systems. Parts of the concept provide for intelligent products to be involved in their own production.

New technical possibilities always lead to new patterns of attack and attacks – this is clear from all the examples quoted here. Industry 4.0 will also not be exempted from this. Successful information technology attacks here can not only steal detailed production data but also be set to work producing selective faults in processes which are not immediately noticed when, for example, certain production parameters are changed. Just imagine a paint-spraying line in a car factory which works with a faked paint mixture, which leads to the paint peeling off thousands of new vehicles just a few months after delivery. The mandatory recall of the vehicles could cost the manufacturer hundreds of millions or possibly even billions of euros.

If you regard such scenarios as farfetched, please remind yourself of the Stuxnet malware which was used to slow down the Iranian atomic programme. The core of the application was a modified control for the centrifuges necessary for operation which was not immediately noticed but almost paralysed the system. The malware programme code analysed by the security provider Symantec had the effect that the Siemens control units sent manipulated commands to two particular types of frequency converters which can be used for controlling the rotational speed of gas ultracentrifuges for uranium enrichment. This could reduce the system's production yield on the one hand and produce vibrations which can cause damage to the centrifuges on the other (Symantec 2011). Little imagination is required to picture similar processes for other technical systems.

A precondition for the success of such highly complicated attacks is of course the availability of detailed knowledge on the systems to be attacked and how they work – one more reason to keep internal company information locked away. Spying by the competition is possibly not the actual aim but just the beginning of a potentially much larger existence-threatening menace.

Technical vulnerabilities as a target for extortion

What value the business secrets of technology companies can have sometimes only becomes clear years later. At the end of 2007, the mobile phone manufacturer Nokia saw itself obliged to pay several million euros to blackmailers who had access to a small file only a few kilobytes large.

At that time, shortly before the iPhone caused a breakthrough for smartphones with touchscreens, Nokia had a market share of around 50 percent with its Symbian mobile phones – in many respects the first smartphones. A so-called encryption key for signing applications had found its way into the hands of blackmailers under mysterious circumstances. If this had been made public, Nokia would have lost control of the installable software – with unforeseeable consequences for the distribution of malware on the devices already sold. Nokia decided to pay and involved the police who were, however, not able to arrest the culprits when the money was handed over.

The case only became public many years later through media reports (MTV 2014) but has not been solved to this day. The police have also lost the trail more than six years after the money was handed over. It was probably not economic espionage in this case: the blackmailers were probably not competitors of Nokia but came rather from a conventional criminal background – if that is at all feasible with cybercrime.

Cybersecurity, cyberwar, cyberactivism, cyberterrorism

If entire infrastructures are endangered by attackers and state protagonists are involved, it is no longer a matter of cybercrime but cyberwar. This is conjured up in various science fiction novels as the warfare of the future: a bloodless but high-loss iteration of the thought of war.

It doesn't require a great deal of imagination to envisage what effect a power failure lasting several days would have on a highly developed country or even just a major city as a result of a cyberattack. Disaster researchers' more or less realistic scenarios range from plundering to conditions akin to a civil war after just a few days without a functional infrastructure. Meanwhile, a number of countries have developed concepts for conducting a cyberwar and are setting up both their own defence centres and attack units. NATO is also involved. The NATO Cooperative Cyber Defence Centre of Excellence (CCDCOE) was established in Tallinn in 2008. Several NATO member states have their own military units focusing on cyberdefence. Interestingly, the civil air traffic control systems in Austria and parts of southern Germany failed at precisely the same time as a NATO cyberwar exercise was taking place in June 2014. It is not clear whether there was any connection between these two events, but the coincidence is alarming in itself.

The big problem with cyberwar is that – like other online attacks – it is not always possible to establish who the real attackers are. Retaliation after a presumed attack can easily hit the wrong opponent, and then an escalation is guaranteed. Moreover, it must be borne in mind that unlike weapons of mass destruction (WMDs), cyberweapons are available not only to states but also to small groups. There is therefore good reason to assume that in the future, not cyberwar but rather cyberterrorism will play a major role in the context of online attacks.

Cyberactivism, also called hacktivism, is a relatively new phenomenon. It involves certain groups pursuing political and other nonmonetary goals by means of hacker attacks, for example denouncing certain business practises. The weapon of choice is data or the publication of confidential or internal company information. It is also conceivable that some operations started under the cover of protest are actually intended to cause damage to a competitor of the actual initiator, who remains in the background.

"Cyberterrorism" is a term heavily discussed, although we have not experienced major attacks yet. Terrorism is, in its broadest sense, the use of violence as a means to create terror or fear, in order to achieve political, religious or ideological goals. Terrorism is considered a major threat to society. Therefore special antiterrorism laws are in place in most countries in the Western world. If we look at cyberterrorism in the same way as we look at terrorism than we would limit it to any cyberattacks that cause real-world harm or severe disruption of the public infrastructure. These are unlikely now but cannot be excluded in the future since, with more and more devices getting connected to the Internet, chances are that some of these can be used against their owners or society. Think about a terrorist hacking attack which purposefully crashes autonomous cars into other cars, uses them as weapons to run over people on the sidewalk or maybe even send bombs to their final destination.

5 En route to the "spy-proof" company

The examples in previous chapters show the developments which spying activities at the expense of companies have undergone due to technical progress, and they also indicate a trend away from classical methods such as bugging, theft or copying documents to new forms which only became possible due to the comprehensive networking of our working world.

It is difficult to express this change precisely in figures due to the large number of unrecorded cases. We can assume with a great deal of certainty that a large proportion of electronic attacks simply remain undetected and therefore that any statistics, wherever they come from, contain figures which are much too low. The chances of receiving valid information are consequently very slim. When deciding to protect your organisation against external threats one should, however, always bear in mind that the reality is possibly much more drastic than the cases we know about would indicate. That is no reason to become paranoid. Caution and healthy mistrust are, however, the order of the day when estimating the risks for your own company.

Recognising risks

Investment decisions within a company are normally driven by numbers. In Chapter 1, I already pointed out the problem of determining a return on investment (RoI) for an investment in company or IT security. By their nature, figures and formulae also dominate when assessing risks.

From a general point of view, risk is a combination of the consequences of a risk event with the associated probability of it happening. In other words, an expectation value for the damage occurring is determined and set against the costs of repelling the threat. If the costs for security measures are less than the expected extent of the damage, the measures are worth it – or at least that is the theory. However, figure-driven analysts often overlook that the initial status is anything but clear; that is to say, the data which flows into such calculations is anything but valid and at best represents an approximation of reality. It is also frequently overlooked that not simply financial and temporal losses define the extent of the damage but that the possible loss of reputation also plays a large role. The assessment of these secondary risks is extremely problematic.

As a simple example for the assessment of risk not associated with espionage, let us take the dilemma of a service station owner: from official police statistics, the owner knows that the risk of a service station being held up is 10 percent per year with an average loss of US$10,000 per year. A protection system may then cost a maximum of US$1,000 per year − if this system can be expected to reduce the risk of a holdup to zero. But if the risk only decreases by half, to 5 percent, the security measures may not cost more than US$500 if they are to pay off.

This extremely simplified example already clearly shows how difficult such calculations are: how do we know, for example, what a holdup will actually cost? What possible effects should we include in our deliberations, and is a loss figure of US$10,000 included in our assumptions? The following points would need to be borne in mind: the amount of money stolen, the goods stolen, the time lost, the reduced turnover, the increased rate of sickness amongst traumatised staff and so forth. The side effects of the security measures have not yet been considered: who do we put off as customers with the new security measures, what effect do they have on staff and their work behaviour and so on? Such effects can be clearly seen at service stations which have introduced night counters as a countermeasure against theft and holdups where customers complete transactions at a kind of security window. The consequences are significantly reduced sales in the shop, ironically the area which brings in a much higher profit margin compared to fuel sales.

This example already shows the fundamental problem with calculating security risks in the real world. The assessment of the risks of industrial espionage, especially cyberespionage, is even more difficult. As already mentioned, despite all the studies there is no really valid data on actual successful attacks. Even less data is available to measure the success of countermeasures. Information from the IT sector, not usually known to miss an opportunity to magnify dangers, is shockingly sparse in this case. That is not surprising: only the costs of individual security measures can be precisely stated.

A purely mathematical approach ultimately reaches its limits if we also wish to include the possible costs of a loss of reputation. If a particularly large amount of damage is done and also becomes public, millions in losses can ensue whilst the probability of this is extremely low. But precisely how low is this risk? 1 to 1,000, 1 to 10,000 or rather 1 to 100, if technical progress is taken into account when calculating the level of threat? Depending on which percentage value is assumed, an investment of €100, €1,000 or even €10,000 may be an appropriate investment sum against €1 million of damage in order to repel this specific risk. Of course, this does not mean that such analyses are of no value. But there are two important conclusions:

- Do not be taken in by false precision when calculating risks. Use the results as a rough guideline only but never as a precise measure for your decisions.
- Do not trust any analyses which come from security suppliers and service providers. They interpret the data to their own greatest benefit.

You should also be aware that even the most sophisticated yield calculations cease to have any significance as soon as judicial responsibility is involved. You should therefore always take the current legal situation into account with risk prevention or reporting possible cases. If members of the board of management do not take this into account, they have to take personal liability, although this liability varies wildly from country to country due to differences in jurisdiction.

Recognising enemies

Beyond the mathematical questions already discussed it is a good idea to bear in mind individual risk factors. These include:

- sector-specific risks, especially in armaments, aerospace, microelectronics, chemicals, pharmaceuticals, genetic technology or financial services;
- company-specific risks taking into account the competitive situation and the position on the world market;
- individual vulnerabilities with regard to the local situation, the environment and the target which under certain circumstances can make individual general risk assessments obsolete by overlapping them; the attackers and their motives always play a key role.

The motives of attackers

As is the case everywhere, when it's a matter of criminal behaviour – and that's what espionage with the aim of achieving advantages over the competition amounts to – the first question, before countermeasures are discussed, has to be, what are the motives of an attacker?

The dominant main motivation for most acts of espionage at the expense of companies is the search for financial advantages. These can be obtained in various ways. The direct competitor possibly looks for details of new technological developments or concrete plans for the market launch of a newly developed product. Here, the motive is quite clearly the possibility of reducing a company's own development time and costs and to adapt its own market activities precisely to the competition. Considerable amounts of time and money can be saved by obtaining such information as it is not in the public domain.

The calculation mechanisms or the calculation of a concrete offer can also be of interest, for example when it has to do with positioning for a public tender, for example in the aircraft industry, with rail traffic or in the construction industry. Whoever wins the contract is financially successful and at the same time can fully exploit the pricing framework. Even companies which are not direct competitors can profit from spying, for example if they receive information relevant to the stock market before the public and practically engage in insider dealing with it.

For spies or tip providers from within the company itself who supply the attacker with information or make access possible, financial enticements are the main motivation, sometimes even in combination with other personal motives. A lack of professional recognition or being overlooked for promotion can trigger a wish for revenge. This prepares the ground for the theft of information or drives the dissatisfied employee to offer his or her services together with interesting internal company information to the competition. Further financial enticement is often unnecessary.

The consulting company Gallup regularly conducts a study on employee satisfaction amongst the employees in different countries and uses it to determine the engagement index – sometimes with worrying results. Gallup has been tracking employee engagement since 2000. The term "employee engagement" is used differently among both academic researchers and human resource managers. In general, it can be defined as the emotional commitment the employee has to the organization and its goals. This implies that work outcome is correlated with employee engagement. In a 2016 published report called "The Worldwide Employee Engagement Crisis" (Gallup 2016), notes that employee engagement has barely budged in years. The researchers also point out that measuring engagement is not a sufficient way to improve it. Even in countries were engagement is relatively high, like in the United States, about half of all employees are not engaged. Gallup further notes that 71 percent of all called Millennials are actively disengaged at work.

Elsewhere, this condition is known as inner resignation – a condition which causes a certain receptiveness for attacks from competitors. Similar studies by other consulting companies with similar findings, as well as in academic research, can be found.

Conduct which can be described as thrill seeking, such as when one thinks "let's see if I can get away with this", should by no means be ruled out. This would declare the sometimes-laughable amounts paid for passing on internal company information in some of the few cases which are discovered. Beyond financial motives and a possible need for a thrill, another extremely worrying development which is currently escalating and needs to be seriously observed is the sabotage of companies or their ability to produce and supply. Here again, dissatisfied employees represent an especially high risk.

Attackers and forms of attack

If the culprit is not caught red-handed at the scene it is often difficult to conclusively establish their identity. The Industrial Espionage 2014 study by Corporate Trust (Trust 2014) attempted to look into this and asked companies whether there had been clues as to the perpetrator with such security incidents.

Unfortunately, corporate trust only asked companies in Austria and Germany about their experiences, but since this research work is more or less unique with its focus on corporate espionage, the core findings are listed here (Table 5.1). Similar outcomes can be expected in other European countries.

Strictly speaking, the term "hacker" does not represent any specific designation of origin but merely refers to the form of the attack. A competitor, a

Table 5.1 Corporate espionage comparison (Austria/Germany)

	Germany (%)	Austria (%)
No, no indication	43.8	38.2
Hacker	41.5	32.7
Customer or supplier	26.8	23.6
Own employee	22.8	30.9
Service provider or consultant	18.3	16.4
Organised crime (gangs)	15.6	14.6
Competing company	14.3	18.2
Foreign intelligence service	5.8	7.3
Other	3.1	1.8
Multiple choices possible		

member of an organised gang or also a curious lone perpetrator can be behind it. Any further assignment is a fundamental problem, as already discussed.

Regarded in conjunction with indications of intelligence service origins, the previous figures (5.8 percent in Germany and 7.3 percent in Austria) could indicate that the threat from intelligence services is not especially large. The results of this and other questionnaires must, however, be viewed with care. Just the differentiation between "private" espionage which emanates from companies and the involvement of state bodies is often impossible from a technical and organisational point of view. Especially in former Eastern Bloc countries, there are many interdependencies between the state and companies which are not transparent for outsiders. Here it may be that a business contact may appear to be a normal private company but can actually be attributed to a state organisation. In such cases it is necessary to rely on conjecture, although the danger is real.

The same Corporate Trust study surveyed the current situation for types of attacks for the same two countries. The following answers were given to the question as to what concrete actions (presumably) took place. The percentages add up to more than 100 percent, as an attack can contain different elements: social engineering, for example, is often just the first step of a large, differentiated attack.

At any rate, this information confirms the assertion of the increasing significance of attacks via the Internet. Cyberattacks, as hacker attacks are also known, are already the dominant method of attack today – with the disconcerting prospect of further growth. In any case, these figures show how priorities need to be set when implementing measures for repelling attacks.

The central problem in assessing these studies remains, however, that only the known attacks are asked about. However, we have to assume that, especially in the area of cyberattacks, most attempted or successful attacks are either only discovered years later or not at all and therefore do not appear in the statistics. As several of the aforementioned examples show, with a cyberattack – that is, an attack via or on the network infrastructure of a company – it is relatively easy to remove all traces and to deliberately blame a third party for the attack.

Table 5.2 Corporate espionage comparison (Austria/Germany), continued

	Germany (%)	Austria (%)
Attacking by hackers on data-processing systems and devices (servers, notebooks, tablets, smartphones)	49.6	41.8
Bugging/intercepting electronic communication, for example e-mails, faxes and so on	41.1	40.0
Social engineering (skilled quizzing of employees on the phone, in social networks and Internet forums, in the private environment, at trade fairs or by own employees)	38.4	18.2
Deliberately passing on information or data and data theft by own employees	33.0	38.2
Leaking data via external third parties (suppliers, service providers or consultants)	21.9	25.5
Stealing IT or telecommunications equipment (PCs, notebooks, mobile phones, smartphones, tablets)	17.4	18.2
Stealing documents, records, samples, machines, components and so forth	15.2	16.4
Bugging meetings or phone calls	7.1	5.5
Other	2.2	1.8
Multiple selections possible		

The role of state attackers

"States have no enemies, just interests." This quote is attributed to various statesmen including Charles de Gaulle and Otto von Bismarck. Whoever said it, it precisely describes relations between states despite all assertions of nation-to-nation friendship by our political leaders, to name but the two most common variants. Diplomatically honed choices of words are to be found everywhere, but when it comes down to the role of state attackers in spying at the expense of companies, elegant restraint is practised. Different terms are used behind closed doors, but it is rare to hear plain words in lectures or interviews by experts from the intelligence services who are responsible for the economic protection of one's country. Since I am German I took my chances and visited several conferences which had speakers from the sector on their agenda. Here is what I got; your mileage may vary, but I expect that you will get similar answers when you ask the experts in your country. As I requested further details from the North Rhine Westphalia's Office for the Protection of the Constitution (North Rhine Westphalia is a federal state of Germany) after the then head of this body had claimed that 96 percent of cases of technology theft affected small and medium-sized companies (Kopplin 2011), I did not receive the details and background I had requested but was fobbed off with a terse reference to the Annual Report on the Protection of the Constitution and other publications. These are, however, normally of little help and formulated overcautiously. In cases of doubt, they do not help with securing a company because they are far too vague. In the brochure titled "Espionage: Are You at Risk Too?" published in March 2014 by the Federal Office for the Protection of the

Constitution, which is directed at companies, the question of who spies on whom in Germany was answered as follows (Verfassungsschutz 2014):

> Nowadays it is difficult to differentiate between friends and foes in the intelligence service world. It can be assumed that many foreign intelligence services are active in Germany to collect information which is relevant for them. If a foreign intelligence service secretly attempts to obtain information this is called spying. In case pf a suspicion, German counterespionage takes measures in every case. Which intelligence service is doing the spying is irrelevant.
>
> However, experience has shown that the intelligence services of certain countries are particularly active in developing espionage activities against our country. The Russian and Chinese services still play a particularly prominent role here.

The official, slick answer to the question as to the danger of economic espionage is (Verfassungsschutz 2014):

> The task description for some intelligence services also includes the protection or promotion of the domestic economy. Insofar, economic and politico-economic questions are. A differentiation should be made between
>
> • science and technology espionage (directed at know-how) on the one hand, and
> • economic espionage in the true sense (directed at economic and company policy and economic and company strategies) on the other.

Although cases of this type repeatedly become known in Germany, directly attributing a concrete leak of know-how – for example to a foreign company – to a foreign intelligence service is often problematic. It can often be a case of spying by the competition – in other words non-state-controlled espionage by a competitor company.

The danger of a company's sensitive information getting into the wrong hands is real in both cases. Innovative, medium-sized companies should especially therefore protect their potential adequately. Insofar as they are sourced from public bodies, the following details represent rare cases of good luck where representatives of the state have hinted at what they know and given a little concrete information.

In most cases, however, the statements are dominated by diplomatic caution and political embellishment. The same holds true for the United Kingdom. In 2012, the then-head of MI5, Jonathan Evans (Evans 2012), issued a warning about the scale of cyberespionage that received extensive media coverage. In a speech he said that a "major London listed company" had lost £800 million as a result of a "hostile state cyber attack", but declined to identify the victim and also did not mention the origin of the corporate espionage attacks.

But looking beyond all the indignation, we should remember one thing: states have always been active in securing economic advantages even by dishonest means. Numerous examples in this book show that this not only was and is tolerated but also actively practised. Sometimes, state involvement is very subtle – for example India's limited recognition of international patents – but the result is basically the same. The following list therefore gives an exemplary overview of the activities of a number of important countries which have been revealed without claiming to be complete. With regard to the countries not mentioned here, it can certainly be assumed that more than a few expend energy on trying to catch up with the technologically and economically leading nations.

China

For years, China has been especially associated with state-driven and economically motivated espionage, and in the meantime this topic is very clearly articulated officially. The president of the Federal Office for the Protection of the Constitution, Hans-Georg Maassen, did not mince his words in the summer of 2014 (Welt 2014):

> Many medium-sized German companies are easy prey. They often find it difficult to identify which of their crown jewels the competition is interested in. [. . .]
> They are competing against a superior opponent. [. . .] The Chinese technical intelligence service alone has 10,000 employees.

You will get similar statements from other representatives of the Western world when it comes to China.

There even is an international consensus that there are several hundred thousand or even a million compliant employees who spy for China's economic benefit. It is no wonder that some companies are unable to cope with adequately protecting themselves.

Unit 61398, a supposed Chinese People's Liberation Army espionage unit, appears repeatedly in this context. A study published by the security company Mandiant in 2013 blamed this group for attacks on 141 organisations, 115 of them from the United States, in 20 sectors since 2006. According to the company, this group, which is between several hundred and several thousand in strength, has the very best technological equipment and its own glass fibre connection from the state-owned China Telecom. According to Mandiant's estimations, Unit 61398 is just one of more than 20 similar groups of attackers in China.

Detailed information however is rare and typically buried in corporate wording and political correctness. In a speech at the Brandenburg service provision conference that I attended on 6 September 2011, Dr Jörg Treffke of the Office for the Protection of the Constitution in the Brandenburg Interior Ministry differentiated between the following Chinese services and responsibilities with a total of more than a million employees:

- Ministry for State Security (MSS): civil domestic and foreign service;
- Military Intelligence Department (MID): domestic and foreign military service in the general staff of the People's Liberation Army;
- Electronic Interception Department (3. VBA): in the general staff of the People's Liberation Army: electronic intelligence;
- Ministry of Public Security (MPS): national police authority.

Similar assessments of Chinese spying activities also come from the United States. In May 2013, the Office of the Secretary of Defence officially announced that China is raising its own technology competence and expertise with the help of investments in other countries – in other words joint ventures – through the deployment of Chinese guest students and researchers and also state-operated industrial and technological espionage. Tom Donilion, Obama's national security advisor, saw Chinese cyberespionage especially as a growing challenge for economic relations with China in a speech before the Asia Society in New York in March 2013. Donilion called on Beijing to investigate and put a stop to these activities (Harris 2014).

Such statements are becoming increasingly concrete and visible. The United States accused China of hacking the Westinghouse company in May 2014 (USAToday 2014). And for the first time, five Chinese citizens were accused of cyberespionage in 2014 (Justice 2014), but the chances of putting any of them before a court are pretty slim. However, the legal action is an important political signal just like the announcement that Chinese participants would be excluded from DEF CON, the world's most important hacker conference, by not issuing them visas (Reuters 2014b). Whether exclusion from events which are often transmitted live is really an effective measure against espionage is doubtful. It is also not known whether these measures came to work in this case.

But is not only the secret formula or high-tech invention that these attackers are after. Coca-Cola was allegedly hacked by hackers who were part of or worked for the Chinese government in 2009. This happened after Coca-Cola attempted to acquire Huiyuan Juice Group, a beverage company based in Beijing. Although everything was on track and the shareholders of Huiyuan were about to accept the deal, the Chinese government had concerns. One seemingly harmless e-mail to Paul Etchells, then the deputy president of Coca-Cola Pacific – that seemed to come from within the Coca-Cola corporation – installed a malware that included a keylogger that captured everything he typed. The attackers were able to monitor a key executive involved in the deal and to transmit confidential data to servers in Shanghai. Chinese officials denied accusations that they were involved in the hacking of Coca-Cola.

On 25 September 2015, an agreement between US president Barack Obama and Chinese president Xi Jinping was made which included the statement that neither government would "conduct or knowingly support cyber-enabled theft of intellectual property" for an economic advantage (Obama 2015). Whether this agreement can be seen as game changer remains unclear. In a report called "Redline Drawn: China Recalculates Its Use of Cyber Espionage" which was published by security company FireEye in June 2016, the authors conclude (FireEye 2016):

> Between September 2015 and June 2016, we observed 13 active China-based groups conduct multiple instances of network compromise against corporations in the U.S., Europe, and Japan. During this same time frame, other China-based groups targeted organisations in Russia and the Asia Pacific region. However, since mid-2014, we have observed an over-all decrease in successful network compromises by China-based groups against organisations in the U.S. and 25 other countries. These shifts have coincided with ongoing political and military reforms in China, wide-spread exposure of Chinese cyber activity, and unprecedented action by the U.S. Government.

It is important to note that FireEye, as well as other security companies and security experts, does not see China's attacks as a monolithic approach but emphasises the role of different groups which may or may not be directly related to the Chinese government. FireEye claims to have identified 72 different groups of hackers in China; other experts come to different estimations. FireEye concludes (FireEye 2016):

> In 2013 [. . .] it seemed like a quixotic effort to impede a persistent, well-resourced military operation targeting global corporations. Three years later, we see a threat that is less voluminous but more focused, calculated, and still successful in compromising corporate networks.

As may be expected, Germany and the United States are not the only targets of China's economic curiosity. There are also reports of attacks on top Russian researchers (Krebs 2012) and Japan is also an important target. And of course there also are reports that China is spied upon by other countries (Japan Times 2017).

Nevertheless, most reports worldwide mention China as the most impor-tant attacker. It is therefore not necessary to wander around in the dark when taking on the threat of China. There are clear indications as to which sectors Chinese intelligence operations are currently particularly interested in. A glance at the current Chinese five-year plan, which was described and documented by KPMG in October 2016, is helpful (KPMG 2016). It lists several emphases: new energies (nuclear, wind and solar power), energy saving and environmen-tal protection, biotechnology, new materials (rare-earth and high-quality semi-conductors), Internet and IT (big data and artificial intelligence), high-quality manufacturing (aerospace and telecommunications) and innovative vehicles (which are operated with clean energy). It also explicitly mentions "following an increasingly clear evolution towards a more sophisticated, better structured and more specialized mode of production" as a main goal (KPMG 2016).

Russia

The Russian Federation's Federal Law No. 5 dated 10 January 1996 titled "Foreign Intelligence" unmistakably declares one of the purposes of intelligence gathering to be "assistance to economic development, scientific and technical progress of the country" (CIS Legislation 2016). Russia doesn't bother with denials or concealment of its intentions behind diplomatic embellishment. Up to 400,000 agents allegedly work for Russia, although this is not confirmed.

Even if the successes of Russian industrial companies are very modest despite espionage, arrogance is totally out of place. It must be borne in mind that Russian computer scientists receive first-class training and – although the pay is still way behind Western standards within the legal IT sector – many succumb to the temptation of working in a cybercriminal environment. In conjunction with the "information provision services" openly provided in Russia by former intelligence service employees, this results in a potentially dangerous mixture on the border between state and commercial espionage.

Ever since the days of the Concorde there was discussion on the role of Russia when it comes to espionage. Just recently, Russian hackers were held responsible for influencing the US election and hacking the Yahoo! user database. But if you limit the research area to industrial or corporate espionage to follow the intention of this book – not much can be found. Public statements from officials are rare.

A report to the US Congress, which combines the collective assessment of 14 American intelligence agencies and was compiled by the Office of the National Counterintelligence Executive, which reports to the director of national intelligence, concludes (DNI 2011): "Russia's intelligence services are conducting a range of activities to collect economic information and technology from US targets." The report also mentions contractual relations that the government in Moscow holds with independent hacker groups to expand their capabilities and cloak responsibility for the computer intrusions.

United States

The revelation of NSA activities by Edward Snowden led to difficulties in relations between Germany and the United States. The bone of contention was that Chancellor Angela Merkel's mobile phone was bugged. Acts of espionage which are directed against commercial enterprises were and are discussed rather less. One of the rare public statements on this is already more than 15 years old: "Of course we spy on you because you constantly pay bribes and we don't." The former head of the CIA, James Woolsey, was quoted as saying this in the *Frankfurter Allgemeine Zeitung* newspaper of 4 February 2001 (FAZ 2001). Other public statements by US representatives suggest that companies are spied upon but allegedly only to combat corruption.

As a reminder, bribery payments abroad were legal in many parts of the European Union and could even be offset against tax until just a few years ago. Anyone who has done business in the Middle East, Africa and Russia can confirm that there is at least a demand for bribery payments and that in many cases no transaction can be concluded without one. Wanting to export one's own views on morality and honesty often does not lead to the successful conclusion of a contract. However, the attitude that business should be kept clean all over the world is not just something the Americans want but now has a consensus all across the Western world.

A number of media reports show that American espionage is not necessarily limited to fighting corruption, for example the case of Ferrostaal, which involves an incident in Nigeria in 2003. This was a major order for radio monitoring systems from Nigeria: the biggest competitor was an American company (DerWesten 2014). As became public from NSA documents thanks to Edward Snowden, major details of the German tender such as price, amount of credit, interest rates and duration were "harvested" by the American Secret Service. Ultimately, the order went to the United States, and Ferrostaal lost US$34 million in turnover (DerWesten 2014).

But it is not only German companies which are threatened by the activities of the American intelligence services. The *New York Times* reported on activities to the detriment of Japanese companies (Sanger 2014):

> As the Clinton administration was in the middle of high-ranking negotiations for an agreement with Japan in the 1990s, it bugged the chief Japanese negotiator's limousine. At the time, the main beneficiaries were the three big American automobile companies and their suppliers.

Brazil also seems to have been affected by espionage activities directed against companies, as President Dilma Rousseff made public in September 2013 (Guardian 2013).

Digging a little deeper, there are even official sources which document American espionage at the expense of companies, for example in 2001 in the European Parliament's "Report on the Existence of a Global System for the Interception of Private and Commercial Communication" about the Echelon surveillance network (EU 2001). Back then, they had the following to say about industrial espionage:

> Whereas the US intelligence services do not merely investigate general economic facts but also intercept detailed communications between firms, particularly where contracts are being awarded, and they justify this on the grounds of combating attempted bribery; whereas detailed interception poses the risk that information may be used for the purpose of competitive intelligence-gathering rather than combating corruption, even though the US and the United Kingdom state that they do not do so.

The Echelon programme is officially ended, and the NSA also maintains that it does not engage in industrial espionage, but even if US officials are to be believed, this raises a question: what about subcontractors to the intelligence services? It should not be forgotten that Edward Snowden was also an employee of a private company that worked for the NSA and was able to access top-secret documents with relative ease. It would be naïve to assume that other employees of private companies did not have similar access authorisation which they can use to provide their domestic clients with internal information from foreign companies. With the large number of external employees working for the American intelligence services, this is not only conceivable but also extremely probable. The problem once again is the same as always with information processing: once data has been collected and stored it leads to new desires and sometimes also to unwanted new kinds of use.

There are in fact former officials who speak plainly in view of Edward Snowden's revelations: William Binney, the former head of technology at the NSA, considers the danger of industrial espionage by the American Secret Service to be thoroughly realistic. He claimed at a data protection congress that part of the data collected by the NSA had been made available to American companies (ComputerWeekly 2015). Edward Snowden himself gave hints about the economically related activities of the NSA when questioned by the European parliament without being specific: "Yes, global surveillance capacities are used daily for the purposes of industrial espionage. It is one of the worst kept secrets in Washington that a main goal of the American intelligence services is to engage in industrial espionage."

Great Britain

Great Britain collaborates closely with the NSA and is also active in the field of economic and industrial espionage with its intelligence services, Military Intelligence, Section 6 (MI6), and Government Communications Headquarters (GCHQ). Media with access to the documents made available by Edward Snowden reported a clear mandate for the English intelligence services to spy "to the benefit of the British economy". Apparently, a kind of division of labour exists with the Americans, and so the British spy, for example, on Italy and share their knowledge with the United States (Spiegel 2013).

There appears to be special competence for monitoring social media platforms: here, the British secret service is in a position to follow events in real time and to draw corresponding conclusions (BBC 2013). According to other sources, their repertoire also includes the manipulation of social media content as well as attacks on websites by generating a large number of simultaneous hits known as distributed denial of service (DDoS) attacks (Guardian 2014) – a toolbox which could also serve to deliberately damage companies.

In 2014, for example, a case became public where several telecommunications companies were spied on by GCHQ. Who the attacks were intended for was not made public, but it is assumed that the customers of the company were the actual targets (Spiegel 2014a).

France

There are strong indications that France engages in espionage with the aim of spying on companies in "friendly" countries. Klaus-Henning Glitza wrote the following in a contribution for Sicherheitsmelder.de in June 2005 (Sicherheitsmelder 2005):

> The French Direction Générale de la Sécurité (DGSE), which is assigned to the French defence ministry, is regarded as the most active and aggressive intelligence service in Germany (but also in the USA and Great Britain) with approximately 3,500 civil and military employees. This service, which is responsible for procuring intelligence abroad, engages in espionage activities with classical spying methods but also with effective telecommunications and electronic espionage similar to the NSA with a global network of some 17 ground stations (officially under the control of the "outsourced" DRM service).

The French weekly *Le Point* wrote the following about this global surveillance system, known in expert circles as the "French Echelon" (Bugbrother 1999):

> The results of this interception – it is not subject to any international law – are handed to the managing directors of a few dozen companies as a confidential message.

Other authors have also found official indications of spying (Ulfkotte 2006):

> In 1990, the DGSE opened the new Special Department No. 7, the "department for large commissions for other countries". More than 20 specialists are employed by this department to obtain as much information as possible about the thousand most important CEOs in the world with which a positive impression could be made or which could be used as a lever for blackmail. Personal preferences, income and hobbies are collected just as much as the names and addresses of their lovers.

There are only a few primary sources, and a lot of what is reported remains mere conjecture. One thing which has often been reported on is, however, curious: there is a special training institution specifically for economic spies, or the École de guerre économique. This is not secret: the school operates an official website at www.ege.fr which since recently is even offered in several languages. There is mention of competitive intelligence training which goes beyond traditional methods. It is up to the individual to decide what to make of this institution.

Germany

Officially, the policy is clear: German intelligence services do not do any intelligence gathering for German industry – that at least is the unanimous picture which is maintained in public. Commentators in the media often complain that the average German is too gullible to act unscrupulously in the interests of the German nation like the rest of the world does (Welt 2013). Other voices recognise here rather an unspoken view of the world which assumes that Germany is much more advanced technologically in many core sectors than the rest of the world and can therefore do without active espionage. With the United States doing well in the software sector and the Chinese acting as a runner-up when it comes to manufacturing technology and automotive products, this seems like a pretty dumb assumption.

Internationally, however, there are completely different opinions on German espionage. In 2005, a book appeared tellingly titled *Spies Among Us: How to Stop the Spies, Terrorists, Hackers, and Criminals You Don't Even Know You Encounter Every Day,* written by the former NSA analyst Ira Winkler. He writes as follows (Winkler 2005, pp. 94–95):

> Although the US government does not typically name it, Germany is widely known to be among the most active intelligence collectors in the world. Germany maintains a very large intelligence organization called the Bundesnachrichtendienst (BND). Although its primary focus was the Eastern Bloc the BND has always engaged in a significant amount of industrial activity. After the breakup of the Eastern Bloc it shifted most of its Cold War resources to industrial efforts. The BND continues to monitor international communications and tries very actively to obtain information that can help German companies.

The book also claims that Siemens, for example, is allegedly supported by infiltrating high-tech companies all over the world. According to Winkler, like the French DGCE, the BND has a strong computer-hacking project with the aim of hacking into computer networks and compromising systems in the worldwide IT infrastructure. This project, which is also known as "Project Rahab", has allegedly existed since the 1990s. Winkler also claimed that the BND has infiltrated the SWIFT international payment system and probably uses its capacities to steal information from private companies.

To what extent this assessment is valid must remain open at this stage as it is more or less just one single opinion.

Collaborations

Another important area of intelligence service is not very transparent: how the services collaborate with one another and with commercial entities. In Germany, the Bundesnachrichtendienst (BND, the German intelligence service) plays an exposed role in this. In 2014, it became known that the BND had passed information to the NSA which it had intercepted at the Frankfurt Internet node between at least 2004 and 2007. However, any attempt to reconstruct the activities of state spies is often met with statements which have to be weighed up carefully.

In the summer of 2013, the managing director of DE-CIX, the company which operates the Frankfurt Internet node – by their own account the second most important Internet node in the world – bluntly declared in conversation with the *Leipziger Volkszeitung* newspaper (LVZ 2013): "We can rule out that foreign intelligence services are connected to our infrastructure and are siphoning off data." Internet nodes like DE-CIX are so important because the providers exchange data there amongst themselves – so-called peering. In the view of an organisation which wants to intercept the data traffic on the Internet as broadly as possible, such nodes are ideal locations for listening in.

Whether it was actually necessary to ask the BND for help or rather unnecessary is a controversial matter. For many of the international providers which are represented at DE-CIX, such as Level 3, Verizon, BT, Vodafone, Global Crossing, Viatel and Interoute, already support the British intelligence services at GCHQ by spying on their customers (Golem 2013). Telecommunication providers in the United Kingdom are very important when it comes to surveillance since most traffic to and from North America runs through undersea cables terminating in the United Kingdom and is routed to mainland Europe through the United Kingdom. That GCHQ has an especially close relationship with the NSA has been well known since at least the Edward Snowden revelations.

The attributability of attacks

Who was it really? Who bears responsibility for an attack? The answer is easy if it can be proved where the information gained has been used, or if a thief is caught red-handed. With electronic attacks via the Internet it is, however, often extremely difficult or even totally impossible. If an attack is discovered, it falls to IT forensic experts to secure appropriate clues. But even if numerous clues indicate a particular origin, for example the IP address, the language of the source code or the time of the attack, it is by no means clear where the attacks actually came from. Expert attackers can lay almost unlimited red herrings and simulate an attack from China or Russia but really be operating from Greenland or South Africa. The *Christian Science Monitor* devoted itself to this problem back in 2010 on the occasion of massive attacks on the American oil industry which appeared to originate from China (CSM 2010):

> The thirst for oil is no proof that a country spies on companies. Even the realization that data [. . .] has flowed to China is not proof but can also be caused by the spying unit of a third country which uses Chinese servers to cover its tracks. [. . .] It is difficult to impossible ever to establish who was actually behind the attack.

Experts come to similar conclusions in other cases in which spying took place via the Internet. As an example, the massive cyberattacks on the German aeronautics and space agency DLR in which Trojans for various operating systems were used should be mentioned at this point (Spiegel 2014b):

> IT forensics experts from the Federal Office for Information Security (BSI) discovered Chinese characters in the code of several Trojans and recurring typos which point to attackers from the Far East.

Even so, there was nothing more than clues, and experts familiar with this case consider attacks by the United States to be just as likely.

The same goes with every other cyberattack. Did Russia really hack the US election in 2016? If you take a close look at the available reports, there is no easy answer, although someone clearly hacked the Democratic National Committee (DNC) and published internal information which may or may not have had consequences for the outcome of the election.

What we really learned from this case is that the security system of the DNC was just too weak and they should have done better securing their internal information.

How to recognise dangers

The examples mentioned in previous chapters show the variety of patterns of attack. In many cases it is, however, usually too late by the time an attack is noticed: a big order has then perhaps long been awarded to a competitor. There are, however, numerous warning signs which do not guarantee that a danger has been recognised in time, but in many cases they provide the right clues. Typical warning signs are, for example:

- Lost orders. The company takes part in a number of tenders and notices a reduction in contracts awarded.
- Unexplained break-ins. The company head office, a subsidiary or a home office is broken into but it seems as if nothing was taken.
- Unsolicited service staff. Maintenance technicians, workmen or service staff come onto company premises without being called for.
- Dust from drilling. There is dust such as is produced by drilling into walls, ceilings or floors, but it is not clear where it has come from.
- Tools not tidied away. Service or repair tools are left lying around unattended in the offices of important employees.
- Parked vehicles. Neutral delivery vehicles and vans park for an unusually long period of time in the direct vicinity of company premises or a residential building where a member of management or important employees live.
- Unexpected presents and prizes. Employees receive unexpected presents which are either intended for use with their PC, for example a computer mouse, or which need a power supply, for example a radio alarm clock or

an extension lead. The same applies to supposed prizes in competitions which nobody has entered.

- Surprising finds. Employees find USB sticks on the car park or elsewhere.
- Open secrets. Third parties are aware of internal company information and development activities although they should not know about them.
- Surprise guests. Unknown persons suddenly appear during secret negotiations in remote hotels or other meeting points.
- Vanished equipment. Notebooks, smartphones or tablets are no longer precisely where they should be after a brief absence, for example a business trip, or vanish temporarily.
- Empty batteries. The rechargeable battery in a mobile device is empty much sooner than usual.
- Slow computer. A computer reacts slower than expected to keyboard entries or programme calls.
- Strange file attachments. Employees receive an e-mail with an attachment apparently from a contact they know. Nothing seems to happen when the attachment is opened; the supposed document is not displayed or does not contain what was promised.
- Open doors. The door lock feels different from usual or is unlocked, even if it was definitely locked before leaving the room.

Every change in small but important details in the surroundings can indicate attacks on your company. But there are not always definite warning signs – see in particular the example of Nortel (p. 56).

Employees as a risk factor

Employees – whether as perpetrators or as stooges for third parties – are involved in a significant proportion of cases of espionage. Some experts I spoke to assume up to 70 percent of all incidents whilst others talk of "just" 20 percent. This fact should definitely be taken into account in your security measures.

A very useful classification model can be derived from an official document of the Landesamt für Verfassungsschutz (LfV), an entity of the Bavarian government, since its approach is not limited to German or continental Europe but aims at international organisations.

It describes three categories of employees that represent an especially high risk for companies (LFV 2013):

- trainees;
- frustrated employees;
- employees whose contracts have been terminated and who remain in the company during their notice period.

The first group are trainees, who collect sensitive data whilst completing their practical and which take this data with them as a kind of present to a competitor where they apply for a permanent job. The LfV therefore recommends only granting severely restricted data access to company data and only to allow access to company data under supervision. The second group concerns employees who feel themselves overlooked at work or are discontented. According to the LfV (LFV 2013), it can often be observed that they take sensitive data with them to help get a job with the competition. Only fundamental human resource management measures can help here.

The last group identified as being problematic are employees who have been given notice and who remain in the company during their notice period. Here too, access rights are often exploited to take important data along as a present for the new employer. For this reason, the LfV recommends immediately limiting or even cancelling access rights in the case of termination and if necessary to completely release the employee from their work. Alternatively, they should be deployed in an area where they have no access to sensitive company data. In American companies, employees who have been given notice are frequently given only a few minutes' time, sometimes under the supervision of security staff, to pack their private belongings and leave the premises. This is a practise which may sometimes be for good reasons and which can also make sense in individual cases, especially in security-relevant areas.

Internationality as a risk factor

Information security must not stop at corporate or national borders. Internationally active companies especially must be aware that information losses from foreign subsidiaries, group companies or business partners not only are feasible but also happen often enough – simply because comparably high employee loyalty cannot be assumed.

But companies which operate exclusively in their home country should also check out their service providers carefully with regard to possible information leaks. This applies as much to the selection of legal and tax advisors as it does to selecting IT service providers and IT services such as cloud computing or managed networking.

The risk of targeted attacks

If security incidents in which cyberespionage was involved are analysed, a pattern which security researchers call an advanced persistent threat (APT) appears ever more frequently. This refers to attack patterns which are directed against individuals or groups of employees and, for example, ask them in an e-mail to click on an attachment or go to a particular website. Unlike the usual spam e-mails with forged phone bills or other irritations, such individual threats appear to come from direct contacts and mostly have a personal reference. The victim's range of interests has already been checked out beforehand – not infrequently by means of their social media activities.

The security provider FireEye describes the risk in its "Advanced Threat Report" (FireEye 2012): according to this, the number of such cases of malware which bypass conventional security systems is strongly increasing. The attack volumes differ substantially depending on the sector, with the most growth being in the fields of health technology and energy. Limited-use domains are increasingly used to outwit conventional security measures; that is to say, the attack is guided to a server which is only used temporarily from which the malware is downloaded. The growth in the number of infections is especially worrying: FireEye recorded a rise of almost 400 percent in a year-to-year comparison.

Protecting your know-how

What information is really important for your company and what must not fall into the hands of a competitor under any circumstances? Possible examples are customer lists, production processes, design plans, development documents, marketing plans, employee files, financial data, calculation schemes, confidential financial data, invoice data and so forth. A major but often-overlooked matter when securing internal company data against unauthorised access is the definition of actual security requirements. Concretely speaking, this means that information which is critical to the company and its availability, confidentiality and integrity (unchangeability) must be dealt with separately.

This is a perception which runs contrary to conventional conceptions of company security. Traditional models differentiate between the inside and outside and attempt to secure this border by technical means. Amongst experts, this is known as "perimeter security". With classical campus security, doors, walls and fences are the main elements of perimeter security, and in the area of IT security, firewalls, as well as content security and antivirus software, attempt to maintain control of the border. It is a struggle which can hardly be won with conventional means any more, especially in the area of IT security.

This also has to do with the increasing spatial fraying of companies: ever more employees no longer work at one fixed location but in a branch, at home or on the move. At the same time, company data is accessed with many different devices which are no longer solely under the control of the company but which are often also used privately. Mobile devices like smartphones and tablets are often under private ownership of the employee and are just used to access corporate information. Until recently this was heavily promoted as "bring your own device" (BYOD). BYOD did not catch on in the Western world except in start-ups and advertising agencies but is very common throughout Asia where it is the norm rather than the exception.

Furthermore, service providers or external employees are increasingly granted access to company data. Certain services, for example cloud computing, also require at least a partial opening up to the outside. It is now in fact almost impossible to define any kind of meaningful outer border which needs defending.

The threat situation is therefore becoming ever more critical as even security software providers harbour certain doubts about the performance of their own systems. This becomes particularly clear when a major player in the sector such as Symantec publicly states that "antivirus is dead" and has lost its raison d'être. Behind this is the simple recognition that conventional antivirus software no longer manages to repel constant new variants of computer viruses within ever shorter periods of time.

In his blog, the security expert Brian Krebs describes details of a highly collaborative cybercrime sector in which the automated testing of newly produced malware against conventional antivirus software is a regular occurrence and where the product is optimised until it functions unnoticed (Krebs 2014). The losers are the providers of antivirus software, and especially their customers, who have to expect strongly decreasing detection rates and ever higher risks.

Employees themselves are no great help, as experience shows they love to click on e-mail attachments despite all warnings about forged e-mails. In other words, a company security expert is well advised to be prepared for this situation and assume that attacks cannot be reliably repelled at the border.

Systems which monitor internal network traffic and trigger an alarm in case of deviations in the usual patterns can be useful. A number of examples in this book indicate that in many cases it is possible to at least detect and stop data leaks even if it is not possible to prevent them in advance. However, it is not a satisfactory answer to the question of protection requirements, and for that reason we need a completely different approach to the problem. Firstly, we must accept that against the background of universal networking and the development of malware with constantly new attack patterns IT security can never be 100 percent guaranteed.

The core problem is that the attacker just needs to find one weakness in your IT security one time and exploit it. But you have to get everything right all the time to successfully protect your corporate assets. What to do?

Since almost every company has confidential data which must be protected at all costs, the answer can only be to separate this out from the normal company way of handling data and treat it separately. In practise, this affects around 3 to 5 percent of all documents, materials and information.

For a construction company it can, for example, be their basis for calculations which needs to be especially protected, whilst processes, machines and staff resources are available to the competition anyway and do not permit any differentiation. This calculation can now be run on separate computer systems which are not connected to the Internet either directly or indirectly. The calculation results – the quotations and lists produced – can then be printed out locally and delivered personally to the addressees in sealed envelopes by couriers. Such a procedure greatly increases the security level for this critical company area and at a justifiable cost if the cost is set in relation to typical project sizes in the construction sector. Comparable models can be provided for other sectors or companies and their individual protection needs.

But reliable protection comes not just from technical measures which in fact result in network or system separation. It is just as important to allow employees in sensitive areas access only to such information which they absolutely need to fulfil their tasks. The distribution of knowledge across several people without individuals having an overview of everything and the limitation of access facilities to the necessary level are important, for example with sensitive research projects and patent developments. It goes without saying that all employees who work in security-critical areas may only do so following a thorough security check.

In a way, these recommendations contradict what has been propagated in social media in recent years: there, talk was and is of opening up – more internal access, more dialogue, more openness and more transparency. However, a meaningful social media strategy should in any case recognise the protection needs of a company and treat it differentially. Fortunately, many social media strategies are meanwhile looking at this necessary internal area of conflict. I have analysed more than 50 social media guidelines and set up various models for different protection requirements in the process (Koehler 2011). I find it is possible to provide more security around core knowledge and at the same time be more open in the overall concept. A precondition for this is the close collaboration of IT security officers and those responsible for social media.

Location-based protective measures

Despite all reasonable fears and the resulting protective measures to do with network security, the classical securing of company premises must not be neglected under any circumstances. This mainly involves:

- constructional access security, such as fences, gates, doors and locks;
- authorisation for access points, such as security guards and reception;
- building and grounds surveillance, such as video cameras and security guards;
- refuse disposal, such as high-quality document shredders for paper waste, permanent destruction of data carriers and so forth;
- procurement and maintenance of extrasecure facilities, such as bug-proof conference rooms and limited-access research-and-development facilities.

These measures should really be self-evident, for without them even the best IT security measures are of little use.

Organisational protective measures

Organisational measures relate to all requirements met by company management to protect against espionage. One important aspect of this is visitor arrangements. Various increments and combinations for this are conceivable.

It is fundamentally recommended that visitors are never allowed on to company premises or into the building unattended. A fundamental ban on allowing visitors into offices also makes sense: they should only be permitted to use certain conference rooms and separate parts of the building. A visitor who is briefly left unsupervised in an office can also cause considerable damage if they take the opportunity to inspect documents left lying around, attack IT systems or install a bug. External workers should be similarly supervised on the premises.

It is not, however, practicable to accompany cleaning staff, but they should at least be supervised by the works protection service in high-security areas. These requirements can be supplemented with security instructions or contractual agreements with suppliers and service providers: even if direct enforcement of liability is only possible in the rarest of cases, the agreement of such an arrangement is an important signal to the other party.

Differentiated access regulations for endangered company areas should apply for visitors and employees alike. It is also urgently necessary to grant employees access only to information on a need-to-know basis in areas in special need of protection. Furthermore, separate guidelines are necessary for marketing and sales, as these groups come into contact with new developments at an especially early stage but mostly have less sensitivity for dangers than employees in the development department.

A further security measure can be to forego promotional and other gifts and decorative elements. USB devices, power banks, wall clocks, water kettles, model cars, you name it. Almost every technical gift can contain a bug or install malware to compromise your IT. Bringing private electronic devices to work and using them, especially cameras and smartphones, requires regulation. Beyond this, a regulation on how phone calls and the use of notebooks or tablets in public spaces on business trips are to be handled is recommended. In case of doubt, conversations in trains, planes, lounges and other semipublic spaces where a lot of people are present should be avoided at all costs, and confidential information must not be displayed in public on computers, even if screen filters are used. Caution is also advisable in taxis and rental cars. The vehicle may have been prepared or the driver instructed accordingly by the competition. In one case, a customer of the author found out that a limousine driver was paid several hundred euros for letting someone else do the driving for him. This happened with a scheduled airport transfer booked at a local limousine service.

Additional security measures should be considered when travelling abroad and only the most essential data taken along. For my trips to non-EU countries I use a separate notebook which contains no software apart from the usual Office applications and no company or customer data. I store data needed for the trip on encrypted data carriers which I do not let out of my sight and do not leave in a hotel safe or anywhere else. This may appear overcautious, but I know of reports from employees of large companies whose notebooks have been stolen from hotel rooms or whose standard mobile phone batteries have been swapped for ones with integrated eavesdropping equipment. Some of my clients had similar incidents while travelling.

Personal protective measures

Measures in relation to employees begin with recruitment. A thorough check of an applicant's background should also be a matter of course for other reasons. Employment legislation does impose narrow limits here though.

Employee training to sensitise them to possible dangers is an extremely good idea. This training, also known as security awareness training, should not only cover IT security topics but also prepare employees to detect and repel social engineering attacks. A person of trust to whom employees can turn if they notice something suspicious or believe they have been the target of social engineering should also be appointed.

A detailed exit plan for employees who leave the company is recommended. This should specifically include access authorizations for internal company IT systems and mobile devices and also rooms and access to vehicles and other services. In some cases it can make sense to release employees immediately, to accompany from the premises personally and to revoke all access authorization immediately.

With all measures, close collaboration between the human resources department and company security is especially important.

Technical protective measures

Do you know what devices are connected to your network? Do you know what services and applications are running in your network or are currently trying to do so? Do you know who has administrator rights in your company so that they can change or bypass settings? Are the selected settings secure? Are your systems always equipped with the latest updates and your antivirus software signatures always up to date? Are mobile devices managed centrally by a mobile device management system, or do your employees use and install what they want? Do you have a system for constantly monitoring your network activities? Are all programmes used properly acquired from a reliable source, or are individual programmes and software tools of uncertain origin being used? Do you use systems which are no longer maintained by the manufacturer, such as Windows XP? Those are just some of the technical safety questions which you have to ask yourself.

Whilst current firewall and virus protection technology is almost always part of the basic setup, there are further important recommendations which have not yet been implemented everywhere. These include the secure shielding of especially endangered rooms or doing without critical wireless transmissions, for example via wireless keyboards and other wireless devices. The use of high-quality encryption processes for all sensitive applications such phones, faxes, e-mail and others should be standard. It is vital to bear in mind that a communications connection is only secure if all parties use the same equipment or the same software, for example for e-mail encryption or when making calls with a crypto-phone. However, that is probably seldom the case in practise, as communications encryption has not established itself beyond specialised application areas. Finally, a network monitoring system should be established which signals anomalies in network traffic or abnormalities with employee access. These are usually known in the market as intrusion detection, content security or data loss-prevention systems.

The problem with the approach sketched out here is simple: it cannot achieve more than basic protection, and gaps in the system are bound to exist. Fortunately, help is at hand.

Basic IT protection

ISO 2700X as well as BS7799 standards come to mind when discussing security on an executive level. BS7799 was written by the United Kingdom Government's Department of Trade and Industry (DTI) and published by the British Standards Institution (BSI) in 1995 as best practices for Information Security Management. It was later extended with a second part on guidance on how to implement an information security management system (ISMS) and a third part covering risk analysis and management. BS 7799 Part 2 was adopted by ISO as ISO/IEC 27001 in November 2005. These standards are important parts of any IT security strategy, but are of limited use in the context of the risks discussed in this book.

BS as well as ISO standards work with standardised risk assumptions and are therefore only of limited suitability for the challenges discussed here. However, they do supply the basic equipment for a systematic individual risk analysis. Overall, it is a useful toolkit for all companies which want to draw the right conclusions from the insights into the risks of increased networking.

Disconnection from the network as a solution concept

Attempts to turn back technical development are generally rather strange and impractical. "The Typewriter as a Secret Weapon: Fear of Being Spied on Causes the Surprising Comeback of a Technology Long Pronounced Dead" was the headline in the Swiss *Tagesanzeiger* newspaper in July 2014 in its digital section as it alluded to considerations which had originated from the Russian secret service (Tagesanzeiger 2014). The story dealt with the procuring of typewriters as protection against surveillance measures (MoscowNews 2013). Those involved were promptly ridiculed in the media. Indeed, it hardly seems sensible to separate out text production from the many communication processes and secure it in this way – especially when electronic aids, together with their attendant potential for being spied on, are then bound to be used to duplicate the papers afterwards.

There are reports that the American author George R. R. Martin, known for *Game of Thrones*, writes his stories on an old DOS computer with WordStar 4.0. He himself regards this procedure as certain protection against computer viruses. However eccentric that may seem, the idea of completely separating important information-processing processes from the rest of the company and therefore also the outside world is a sensible idea which should definitely be included in considerations about handling highly sensitive company data.

This concept of physically disconnecting a computer for security reasons even has a name. It is called "air gap".

It needs to be said that even air-gapped computers are under attack. Compromising air-gapped computers is a kind of fun exercise for security researchers. Over the last few years they have found different ways to successfully attack air-gapped PCs by using FM radio waves, the sound of hard drives and other means of unwanted communication channels.

In most cases, the attackers need an insider that wittingly or unwittingly transfers the attack code via a data carrier, usually a USB drive.

Hacking as a defensive measure

Should companies employ hackers? This is a company protection question which has been discussed a great deal. The thought behind it is that if a company is attacked, it could defend itself and launch a counterattack with its own hacker, similar to the concepts known from the armed forces. After all, everyone has heard of white-hat hackers who are on the right side, unlike black-hat hackers. This consideration is therefore as self-evident as it is unfeasible in practise: apart from legal risks, there is a really acute danger of pursuing the wrong party and possibly attacking innocent bystanders. In practise, it also may well be difficult to react at precisely the right moment.

Hacking is, however, justified when testing security measures. Here, a team of people who can systematically test security measures for their effectiveness and correct configuration with penetration tests are needed rather than one single hacker who is perhaps a specialist in just one particular area of information security. Such tests should always be supplemented with social engineering attacks which test the organisation, as with mystery shopping.

Cyberinsurance

Special insurance policies play virtually no role when talking to company directors about measures they have taken to defend the company against information leaks. That is surprising as in many other company areas insurance policies are now standard, for example for the personal liability of management where what is known as directors' and officers' (D&O) insurance covers such risks.

Cyberinsurance is intended to cover corresponding financial risks from security but is little known in the corporate world to date. A cyberinsurance policy, also referred to as cyber risk insurance or cyber liability insurance coverage (CLIC), is designed to help an organisation if a security event occurs. It does so by mitigating risk exposure by offsetting costs involved with recovery after a cyber-related security breach or similar event. Cyberinsurance can be traced back to its roots in errors and omissions (E&O) insurance. Cyberinsurance is a relatively new offering from the insurance industry; it first became known at around 2005. According to PwC, in 2015 about one-third of US companies currently purchased some type of cyberinsurance (PWC 2015). Other countries are lagging behind, but the US numbers show that organisations are seeing a need for cyberinsurance. While there is no standard for underwriting these policies, the following expenses are typically covered:

- forensics investigation to determine what happened, which may include the services of a third-party security firm;
- business losses, which typically includes but is not limited to monetary losses due to network or system downtime, business interruption, data loss recovery and costs involved in managing a crisis, which may involve repairing reputation damage;
- legal expenses associated with the security event, including regulatory fines;
- extortion, or paying for ransomware recovery keys.

Cyberinsurance coverage and premiums are based on an organisation's industry, type of services provided, data risks and exposures, security posture, policies and annual gross revenue.

Cyberinsurance has a fundamental problem: how should the current security level be assessed as a basis for classifying the insurance? Whilst the possible amount of loss is relatively easy to quantify, the probability of loss – as the second main measure for determining the insurance premium – is not so easy to calculate because the influence of internal security measures is too great. The number of actuarial features for insuring a truck are straightforward – after all, the Ministry of Transport (MOT) test, an annual test of vehicle safety and exhaust emissions required in Great Britain, ensures technical safety – but this is not the case for cyberinsurance.

From the perspective of this book, it is also important to mention that the losses by cyberespionage are difficult to track and sometimes occur the year after the security incident happened or is detected, so even if corporate espionage is explicitly included in your contract, this does not mean that insurance is the solution to the risks you are facing in this case.

At best, the insurance premium is calculated by means of – normally expensive – professional opinions by experts who specialise in security reviews. There is currently no certification body to check the suitability of an IT infrastructure for secure participation in Internet traffic, and due to the complexity and diversity of the security solutions on the market and the possibilities for combining them, there is not much prospect of one being established. It would, however, be conceivable for an insurance company to draft standards in consultation with leading IT sector companies. Such models consisting of standardised technology and tailor-made insurance protection will be the future – if only because the liability risks for management as a result of data leaks are becoming ever more unmanageable.

Maybe you will even get the insurance as an add-on if you order a special service package.

Social media and the like

One of the most controversial topics when it comes to protecting a company against information leaks is the desired degree of openness towards the outside world. The discussion about the use of social media especially propagates an extensive opening up and transparency which is doubtlessly to be regarded positively in marketing and personnel recruitment terms but at the same time makes companies vulnerable to social engineering attacks.

To what extent employees in key research and development positions should have a presence in corresponding social media activities is a matter of controversy. It is clear that every appearance and every statement by such a person in public networks makes it easier for attackers to study and infiltrate the company and its structures. It is not just industrial espionage which represents a danger for companies: sometimes it is "just" a headhunter searching for people with certain skills who damages a company in this way – completely without any hint of espionage but possibly just as effective.

One should not talk of paranoia here; in the age of Facebook, LinkedIn and other social networks, it is hardly possible to keep anything confidential about internal staff structures. But if a critical debate helps to identify and secure protectable know-how in the heads of employees, then it is extremely important for the continued existence and market success of a company. Sometimes the suggestion is made in this context to do without not just social media but also business cards with titles and e-mail addresses – not a good idea. Such "security measures" are unlikely to hold up a motivated attacker but make dealing with legitimate business partners more difficult.

There are no clear recommendations for handling social media in these times of threat by economic and industrial espionage. In any case, it is important that employees receive clear guidelines for handling social media. The regulations in the form of social media guidelines introduced in many companies should in any case reflect the individual situation of the company, for example the relevance of research and development work for company success or the concrete threat situation due to being part of a certain sector.

In the summer of 2012 a research team from University of Augsburg in Germany published a paper titled "Social Networks and Their Effects on Company Security". The paper was published with governmental support. It brings together helpful tips for company and security officers (Augsburg 2012). The core principle outlined in this document is simple but nevertheless important: what is confidential should remain confidential and internal matters should always remain internal. It is important to point out to employees what information is to be treated openly and what is confidential or top secret. The paper emphasises the significance of written employee guidelines for social media. For example, the most important rules include never using the company password for accessing a social network – something which really should go without saying. The content of enquiries and messages, especially friend requests from unknown or allegedly known persons, should not simply be trusted but always treated with caution. The same applies to messages with unusual content: they must never be allowed to lead to blind clicking on links or opening of any attachments.

It is better anyway to not post any very private or intimate details or pictures on social media channels so as not to make yourself too much of a target. The private sphere settings should be selected accordingly so that as little information as possible is accessible to third parties. To check this, the authors of the study at the University of Augsburg suggest regularly googling yourself – searching for your own name and your own presence online. This helps to ensure you do not become easy prey for potential attackers. This advice from the University of Augsburg actually goes beyond the actual core problem by also attempting to regulate the fundamental handling of social media but it is still helpful for sensitising to the problem both employees and managers who do not have further prior knowledge.

Companies which work mainly with young employees often think they are safe because they just assume that anybody who has grown up with digital media has automatically developed a high degree of competence in dealing with the risks. This estimation is wrong, or at least that's what a research report by the Milan-based Tech and Law Center shows. In this interdisciplinary institution, digital technologies and their relation to law and society are investigated. In the "Security of Digital Natives" research report, the sense of responsibility of the Internet generation for security online was investigated (TechAndLaw 2013). The highly readable cybercrime blog at the Police University of Brandenburg concisely summarises the research results as follows (Cybercrimeblog 2014):

> One important finding of the project is that a sense of security and responsibility does not automatically develop amongst young people if they have grown up with digital media. With many of the students surveyed, the scientists discovered a serious lack of knowledge about using protection options as well as a lack of will to use known possibilities insofar as the protection solutions are not especially simple from a technical point of view.

If you occupy yourself with social media in the context of company security, you are advised not to forget old-school media. Whether, for example, the local paper really has to print the ranking list of the company bowling tournament from which an organisational chart can be more or less simply inferred is certainly a matter of doubt. Caution is therefore also required when dealing with media representatives and with those who claim to be media representatives, for the latter is a long-proven attack route for competitive intelligence professionals and industrial spies.

But even if you get everything right by finding the right balance between social media-induced openness and security once, you cannot be sure that it stays that way. Social media platforms constantly tweak the way they are working and using the customer data, which can lead to unintended consequences when it comes to protecting your corporate assets.

For example, in April 2017 some LinkedIn users who had the LinkedIn app installed on their iPhones found the following message on their screens: "LinkedIn would like to make data available to nearby Bluetooth devices even when you're not using the app. We will help you connect with others that are nearby."

No further explanation was given to the users. You can only guess what this new feature is all about. One scenario would be that you get the names, contact information and other details of random people riding the same subway train, eating in the same restaurants or waiting in the same security line at the airport. Another scenario would be that LinkedIn only uses this information to show you if anyone who is on your contact list nearby.

After a public media uproar, LinkedIn issued the following statement (The Register 2017a):

> To help our members more easily connect with one another, we're exploring an opt-in "find nearby" feature that will help them find other members nearby. This will be an opt-in experience and members will have control of when their location is used for this feature. A prompt to enable Bluetooth on our iOS mobile app went out in error to a small group of LinkedIn members. (This group included at least one Tom's Guide staffer.) We are working on a fix immediately and we apologize for any confusion.

For now there seems to be no reason to worry, but expect similar "incidents" to happen in the future since all major Internet companies have a history in propagating new "features" without asking. They will only backpedal if they are caught red-handed.

Rebound effects

We are all familiar with self-made security vulnerabilities. Post-it notes with the password stuck to the edge of the screen or under the keyboard, a wedge under the door to the side exit which is used for cigarette breaks: many weak spots are home-made – and unnecessary. Password management which demands long and complicated passwords which must be changed regularly positively forces employees to produce memory aids. The practise of sending smokers outside to smoke also regularly leads to people making it easy for themselves and simply propping doors open with wedges or something else. On top of this, if the company is so large that not everybody knows everybody else, it may even be that someone politely holds the door open for an intruder.

Similar avoidance strategies also become widespread wherever access control systems do not meet practical requirements – in other words, they are too slow in the view of employees. This is often the case with biometric systems where identification by means of a fingerprint can take several seconds and employees have the feeling they are being impaired in their work. It is then only a relatively small step for employees from occasionally jamming the door open to sabotaging the door mechanism. For this reason, a team of reporters succeeded in bypassing all security mechanisms and gaining access to the runway at Tegel Airport in Berlin, still the main airport of the German capital (Focus 2012).

Deference to authority in many companies is almost as big a problem – nobody wants to lock out the company management. Clothes make the man, so to speak, as they have done for centuries. I have frequently experienced this. One case involved the subsidiary of a large technology company which I visited at irregular intervals some years ago. If I arrived dressed in jeans and a polo shirt, the security service which operated the reception desk was regularly alerted and I always had to wait to be collected by the person I had come to visit. If I turned up in a suit and tie, however, I was simply buzzed through the access door without further ado. They obviously shied away from scaring off an important executive.

This works similarly with public authorities under certain circumstances. When visiting the Regional Office for the Protection of the Constitution, I was already intercepted at the gate on one occasion and on another I got straight past the entrance barrier in my car. The difference was that one week I was travelling in my own private car, a small, not-very-prestigious Smart ForTwo, and the next I was driving a black Mercedes E-Class with a local registration plate from the regional capital, but both times I wore a dark suit and tie. To salvage the reputation of the Regional Office for the Protection of the Constitution, I should say that I was only allowed to drive on to the premises; to access the building, the identity check and processing were precisely to the usual standards in both cases.

These more or less random experiences clearly show that the old saying "clothes make the man" still applies – especially in situations where it is a matter of company security. There is no doubt that potential attackers also don't come to similar conclusions by chance but also apply them to their actions. An internal company security directive should therefore actively address such topics. I also recommend doing regular tests to keep security awareness high.

Counterintelligence in practise

What should be done if it is foreseeable that company security is in acute danger or an attack has possibly already taken place? Beyond classical technical and organisational steps, a number of further measures are worthy of closer examination.

Disinformation as a strategic option

One of the most successful defensive measures in concrete cases of danger is disinformation. This means giving an attacker the feeling he or she has already achieved the goal. Clues are laid out rather like a honeypot and lead to the wrong stock of documents. However, clumsy forgeries won't work – detailed preparation is needed to be successful. For this reason, a great deal of time, effort and considerable resources are required for a successful disinformation campaign and if necessary the deployment of external experts.

Thomas Alva Edison, the inventor of the light bulb, boasted that he had found numerous ways of not inventing the light bulb. This charming description of his unsuccessful attempts points the way for successful disinformation in research-oriented areas. Here there are always a few failed attempts which are extensively documented and suitable as bait for a disinformation campaign. Design drawings which are prepared with errors in them are also suitable. False information on price strategies or the planning of product launches can equally be used – purposefully forged documents make it possible.

The effect aimed for is that the attacker believes he or she has achieved his or her goal, uses the prepared documents and lands in a dead end. It costs attackers time and money and weakens their competitive position.

Professional help

A large number of service providers strive for company security. Beyond the classical IT security provider, a number of which offer managed solutions which are supposed to secure the network, detect anomalies and raise an alarm in good time, a number of providers specialise in throwing light on security incidents. These include private investigators and large detective agencies which deal with such problems for €1,000 to €3,000 a day according to the spokesperson for the International Federation of Detectives (BID) – with an alleged clear-up rate of 90 percent (Welt 2007).

Whilst detective agencies are typically set on to people – either one's own employees or external spies – other service providers specialise in the technical examination of infrastructures and systems and also the forensic examination of incidents. Considerable costs can accrue in the process due to the high degree of technical effort required, for the service provider has to maintain expensive equipment, for example X-ray machines with which hardware components can be nondestructively checked for manipulation.

Assistance from the government

In many countries, companies which fear they have been spied on can turn to government bodies. The amount of help you can expect varies massively from country to country and probably also relates to your company's importance for the national economy.

For example, in Austria, the Federal Agency for the Protection of the Constitution and Counterterrorism (BVT) is responsible for repelling espionage activities. Their task is described as follows (BVT 1):

> Especially economic and industrial espionage represent a potential threat for the attractiveness and reputation of Austria as an economic centre. Guaranteeing the security of the corporate and research environment in Austria requires the networking of the BVT as the responsible security authority with partners from corporate and university environments. The possibility of direct communication, the provision of relevant and up-to- date information and the mutual creation of knowledge are the basis of the successful prevention of economic and industrial espionage.

A handbook titled *Economic and Industrial Espionage: Expertise Protection Handbook for the Austrian Economy is available* on the website of the Austrian Office for the Protection of the Constitution (BVT 2). It was published back in 2011 but contains a number of useful tips on counterespionage.

In Switzerland, responsibility for economic protection falls to the Federal Intelligence Service (FIS). One of the organisation's tasks is "advising companies, universities and technology centres on possible preventive measures to inhibit illegal activities in the fields of espionage and proliferation". A brochure on the "Prophylax" prevention and sensitisation programme, published in 2010, is available on the Swiss intelligence service website (VBS). This is intended to inform companies how hazards and illegal business can be recognised and prevented. Other European countries have similar offerings.

Other countries act a great deal more aggressively. The US Economic Espionage Act, which was mentioned earlier in this book, aims to prevent the theft of intellectual property by foreign companies and governments. The purchase or possession of company secrets which have been obtained without the consent of the owner thus becomes an offence which can be punished with 10 years' imprisonment or a fine of US$250,000 for each person or US$5 million for each company. Here again, there is still the problem of accountability and also the difficulty of actually catching the perpetrator insofar as they are operating from abroad.

First aid

What should you do if something has happened and you or your company has become the victim of an attack? The most important recommendation is to secure proof immediately as far as possible, if necessary by external specialists and involving state bodies. It is not quite so easy to answer the main questions in such a situation: what has actually happened? How serious is the damage? Who was it? What needs to be done?

What has actually happened and what consequences it has is not always evident at first glance. The example of the network equipment company Nortel clearly shows this: after the company had been spied on, they merely changed the passwords and carried on as usual. As far as we know now, nobody bothered to find out what really happened and made sure that there are no backdoors left by the attackers. This would have been expensive and time consuming. Such a statement is hardly credible immediately after the revelation of a security-related incident and has to be regarded as a kind of public relations emergency stunt. Not infrequently, companies then have to admit the entire extent of an incident and revise their hasty statements weeks afterwards.

In addition, professionals now increasingly obliterate their tracks. After a cyberespionage attack on the design plans for a fighter plane, it was noticed that the perpetrators had installed a programme which encrypted data during extraction. This meant that the experts who investigated the incident could not even precisely establish what data had been stolen. It was even said that the hackers had "tidied up thoroughly" (WSJ 2009). The more professional the attacker is, the more such an approach is to be expected. This even applies to the world's best-financed intelligence service: according to media reports, the NSA itself does not know precisely what documents the whistle-blower Edward Snowden took. The former head of the NSA and the US cybercommander said in an interview with the Australian *Financial Review* that neither the number of documents nor what documents had been taken was known (AFR 2014).

It is often hardly possible to assess how great the damage is for the reasons already mentioned – above all when it is not even clear what has been taken. Also, damage caused by espionage activities is normally only quantifiable if the benefiting competitor uses the stolen documents – in other words, the competitor puts a competing product on the market or surprisingly wins a tendering process. The problem of the difficulty of quantification has already been discussed frequently in this book. The question of who the perpetrators are cannot always be unequivocally answered.

In the end, the question which remains is, what now? A meaningful answer should aim at defining adequate measures which close security gaps on the one hand and on the other prevent spies or their clients from being able to use the stolen information. State bodies and possibly also private investigators should be involved here.

Pillars of corporate protection

To regard security against the leaking of important information as a purely technical problem falls short of the mark. The examples given here show very clearly that IT security begins in people's heads – in every employee's head. Because the decision to open an e-mail attachment, to accept a contact request in a social network or to install a particular app on a smartphone can already have grave consequences for company security, it is decisively important to sensitise employees to possible dangers.

Technical and organisational measures are only of limited assistance. Organisational stipulations must of course support behaviour appropriate to the level of risk. This can include the establishment of a contact person to whom employees can turn quickly and unbureaucratically in cases of doubt. And company security also needs protection systems to the latest technical standard to be installed and professionally maintained, including constant updates and if necessary the decommissioning of software and system environments which are no longer maintained or used. But this alone can only be as good as every single employee, because the examples show nothing more clearly than the significance of an individual decision for the security of the entire organisation.

But does such an exemplary company actually exist? One whose employees always act attentively and prudently, whose rules are structured comprehensively and comprehensibly and whose IT security is always fully up to date in all respects? While coping with change induced by digital disruption? This is most unlikely in practise. It would also possibly not be much help, for so-called zero-day security vulnerabilities which are so new that they are not even known to IT providers and security firms affected can still be exploited. One or two standard attacks would perhaps then be obsolete, but 100 percent security is unfortunately impossible in our interconnected world.

It only remains for us to come to terms with the technical inadequacies of this interconnected world, to invest as much as is reasonable in preventive measures and to be equipped for a possible breach of our security chain – whether this means the disconnection and isolation of especially important areas or by taking out insurance. If the worst came to the worst, this would at least limit the economic consequences for the company, customers and shareholders. But ultimately, the informed, watchful employee who identifies with the company is still the best insurance.

6 The future of economic and industrial espionage

The development of the Internet and mobile communications towards a comprehensive interconnection of our private and working world not only offers new opportunities but also brings new risks. These can even lead to commercial ruin; a targeted and sustained DDoS attack on a company in the online sector could be enough to cause the business model and the company to collapse. Even though such dependencies only affect individual companies in certain sectors, the threat situation also intensifies for all others. The risk of becoming the victim of malicious cybercriminals and unscrupulous competitors has grown especially dramatically in recent years. A new awareness of the risks is needed in order to hold one's ground against these new threats.

In the summer of 2014, the Potsdam Conference for Cybersecurity indicated the best way forward in many cases. There, the state of affairs described in this book was discussed unsparingly and openly by like-minded people from all over the world. It was one of those rare moments where truth about the real state of IT security in the world surfaces and is not immediately covered up with political talk.

Holger Mey, the head of advanced concept at Airbus Defence and Space and also a professor of foreign policy at the University of Cologne, reported that he assumes that hardware and system software are compromised as a matter of principle. He sees particular risks in the purely cost-driven purchasing behaviour of companies and expects that the development of a meaningful awareness for security still needs time. His comparison between the security of companies and the safety of automobiles is simple but impressive: in the automotive sector, it took years before the safety of the product was given high status. In his estimation, companies and their information technology still have some way to go. On the very same day other experts pointed out that attacks against competing companies could be had for just a few hundred euros – at the right point in time, for example during a product start-up – but could still cause considerable damage. But they also asserted that 80 percent of attacks were avertable with the right configuration of existing security technology. None of those attending this conference or any other experts in the field had simple solutions to offer – and they are also not to be had elsewhere. System security has continuously deteriorated in recent years despite all the promises of the IT security industry. The examples in this book illustrate this fact very clearly.

Regarding the fundamental development prosaically, it can be seen that we are in the middle of the Internet revolution and are possibly still right at the beginning. Market researchers and Internet providers expect further strong growth in Internet use: between 2005 and 2018 alone, data traffic in the global Internet will supposedly have increased 64-fold and it is not slowing. By next year, global data traffic of 1.6 zettabytes per year is expected – an inconceivably large figure. An ever-larger part of this will come down to devices connected online without any human interaction. This will bring new, difficult-to-control gaps in control systems for domestic technology, motor vehicles and other objects of our professional and private life which can be exploited by hackers. This Internet of Things will bring with it new security risks for internal company matters.

We have already met a number of these new dangers; the Shodan search engine described in Chapter 4 points the way. The first examples of this new world can already be found in the wild. *Computer World* magazine reported on LEDs which can "listen", in other words eavesdrop, on conversations and transmit them. The bug of the future will then perhaps come with the new energy-saving bulb or is part of a smart domestic-technology control system. That is a frightening prospect – and merely the precursor of a new wave of technologies which need to be closely and critically observed. For even drastic security measures can fail in future: the network separation which has already been discussed as a solution for important confidential tasks would be useless in the case of a development which leapfrogs the "air gap" consciously left between the two system environments.

Those prone to nostalgia have to accept that there is no way back to the pre-Internet era. It is also impossible to predict whether the omnipresent Internet technology and the widely used Windows, Mac OS, iOS and Android operating systems can be replaced with secure network connections and software. The Internet is too widely distributed, the fundamental communications protocols are too unreformable and the software systems invented by humans but no longer understood in detail by them are too complex. A new "Clean Slate Internet" that includes all the security measurements that we are currently lacking so badly will remain a theoretical model of the academic world for the foreseeable future. We will have to get by with what we have at the moment, with all its insecurity and risks. The only sensible reaction to these mainly determinate developments is always to stay on top of things, to actively follow technological developments, to draw the relevant conclusions for your company and to institute the necessary technical, organisational and staff-related measures.

The world of economically motivated espionage has changed in its choice of means and methods but not its aims. Knowledge about the competitor's next product development, their offer prices for the next tender or other sensitive data which promises competitive benefits will remain a strong motivator for spying on other companies – whether under cover of competitive intelligence or as open economic or industrial espionage. Unfortunately, the end also justifies the means here. The temptation is big, and the development of spying on the competition will therefore make progress, whether we want it to or not. So it is better to be prepared for it.

References

AA 2007. Newspaper report, September 18th 2007. www.augsburger-allgemeine.de/sport/Daeninnen-sauer-ueber-chinesische-Spionage-id2968961.html.

AA 2008. Eurocopter: Spionage hat Firma nicht geschadet. Newspaper report, June 19th 2008. www.augsburger-allgemeine.de/donauwoerth/Eurocopter-Spio nage-hat-Firma-nicht-geschadet-id3826001.html.

AFR 2014. Interview transcript: Former head of the NSA and commander of the US Cyber Command, General Keith Alexander, May 8th 2014. www.afr.com/p/technology/interview_transcript_former_.

Airbus 2003. Airbus's secret past. The Economist special report, June 12th. www.economist.com/node/1842124.

Antony, Sebastian 2011. Tens of millions of HP LaserJet printers vulnerable to remote hacking. www.extremetech.com/computing/106945-tens-of-millions-of-hp-laserjet-printers-vulnerable-to-hacking.

Ariely, Dan, Garcia-Rada, Ximena, Hornuf, Lars, and Mann, Heather 2014. The (true) legacy of two really existing economic systems. Munich Discussion Papers 2014–26.

Augsburg 2012. Research paper. www.hs-augsburg.de/medium/download/oeffentlichkeit sar beit/publikationen/2012_07_03/soziale_netzwerke.pdf.

Avast 2016. blog.avast.com/republican-national-convention-delegates-unknowingly-use-fake-wi-fi-networks.

Bayer, Justin K. 2013. AMSC/Sinovel industrial espionage thriller takes a procedural detour, threatening U.S. criminal prosecution. www.lexology.com/library/detail.aspx?g=c06d91c6-1d63-4fb0-a1a7-d803bf90ef60.

BBC 2013. NSA leaks: UK and US spying targets revealed. BBC news report, December 20th 2013. www.bbc.com/news/world-25468263.

Bialik, Carl 2008. About those hundreds of thousands of lost laptops at airports. https://blogs.wsj.com/numbers/about-those-hundreds-of-thousands-of-lost-laptops-at-airports-413/.

BKA 2012. BKA report 2012. www.bka.de/nn_224082/SharedDocs/Downloads/DE/Pub likationen/JahresberichteUndLagebilder/Cybercrime/cybercrimeBundeslagebild2012,te mplateId=raw,property=publicationFile.pdf/cybercrime Bundeslagebild2012.pdf.

BKA 2016. www.bka.de/DE/AktuelleInformationen/StatistikenLagebilder/Polizeiliche Kriminalstatistik/pks_node.html.

Bloomberg 2011. www.bloomberg.com/news/photo-essays/2011-09-20/famous-cases-of-corporate-espionage.

Bolle, Lars 2013. Strafe gegen US-Team wegen Spionage. www.yacht.de/sport/americas_cup/strafe-gegen-us-team-wegen-spionage/a76897.html.

Bruer, Wesley 2015. FBI sees Chinese involvement amid sharp rise in economic espionage cases. http://edition.cnn.com/2015/07/24/politics/fbi-economic-espionage/.

Bugbrother 1999. www.bugbrother.com/echelon/frenchelon.html.

BVT 1. www.bmi.gv.at/cms/BMI_Verfassungsschutz/wis/start.aspx.

BVT 2. www.bmi.gv.at/cms/BMI_Verfassungsschutz/wis/files/Handbuch_WIS.pdf.

BZ 1996. Newspaper report, August 26th 1996. www.berliner-zeitung.de/mit-infrarot
kamera-neue-auto-modelle-fotografiert-weiterleitung-der-bilder-per-satellit-vw-auf-
eigener-teststrecke-ausspioniert-16675150.

Cellebrite 2015. ec2-107-23-31-70.compute-1.amazonaws.com/mobile-forensics/capabili
ties/operations/physical-extraction.

Cerf, Vinton. ec2-107-23-31-70.compute-1.amazonaws.com/mobile-forensics/capabilities/
operations/physical-extraction.

China 2005. Schwerer Fall von Wirtschaftsspionage bei Autozulieferern. www.china-intern.
de/page/wirtschaft/1115198982.html.

Choke 2010. www.spiegel.de/spiegel/print/d-70701753.html.

Churchill 2015. The spectacle of security: Lock-picking competitions and the security industry in
mid-Victorian Britain. https://academic.oup.com/hwj/article-abstract/80/1/52/665007/
The-Spectacle-of-Security-Lock-Picking?redirectedFrom=fulltext.

Cisco 2014. https://tools.cisco.com/security/center/content/CiscoSecurityAdvisory/cisco-
sa-20140110-sbd.

CIS Legislation 2016. cis-legislation.com/document.fwx?rgn=1537.

Citizen Lab 2014. Police story: Hacking team's government surveillance malware. https://
citizenlab.org/2014/06/backdoor-hacking-teams-tradecraft-android-implant/.

Clueley, Graham 2011. Tour de France cheat faces suspended sentence in malware case.
http://nakedsecurity.sophos.com/2011/10/25/tour-de-france-cheat-faces-suspended-
sentence-in-malware-case.

CNET 2007. SAP admits 'inappropriate downloads' from Oracle. News report, July. www.
cnet.com/uk/news/sap-admits-inappropriate-downloads-from-oracle/.

Columbia 2011. University news report (no exact date given). http://engineering.columbia.
edu/can-you-trust-your-printer.

ComputerWeekly 2015. Bill Binney, the 'original' NSA whistleblower, on Snowden, 9/11
and illegal surveillance. www.computerweekly.com/feature/Interview-the-original-NSA-
whistleblower.

Contextis 2014. www.contextis.com/resources/blog/hacking-internet-connected-light-bulbs/.

Cornell n.d. a. Cornell Law School Legal Information Institute. www.law.cornell.edu/wex/
economic_espionage.

Cornell n.d. b. Cornell Law School Legal Information Institute. U.S. Code Title 18, Part I,
Chapter 90, §1839. www.law.cornell.edu/uscode/text/18/1839.

CSM 2010. US oil industry hit by cyberattacks: Was China involved? www.csmonitor.com/
USA/2010/0125/US-oil-industry-hit-by-cyberattacks-Was-China-involved.

Cusick, Daniel 2013. Chinese wind power giant faces U.S. indictment on economic espionage charges. E&E News report, July 23rd 2013. www.eenews.net/stories/1059984847.

Cybercrime Blog 2014. Blog post. http://cybercrimeblog.fhpolbb.de/sichtenweisen-zu-
sicherheit-bei-digital-natives/.

Dark 2010. 'Robin sage' profile duped military intelligence. IT security pros. www.dark
reading.com/risk/robin-sage-pro-le-duped-military-intelligence-it-security-pros-/
d/d-id/1133926.

Deltl, Johannes 2008. *Strategische Wettbewerbsbeobachtung*. Gabler, 2011.

Demsteader, Christine 2005. Ericsson hacker charged with spying. www.thelocal.se/
20050309/1076.

DerWesten 2014. Newspaper report, January 21st. www.derwesten.de/staedte/essen/
nsa-spaehte-auch-essener-firma-ferrostaal-aus-id8895036.html.

DNI 2011. Foreign Spies Stealing US Economic Secrets in Cyberspace (Report of the Office of the Director of National Intelligence to the US Congress) www.dni.gov/files/docu ments/Newsroom/Reports%20and%20Pubs/20111103_report_fecie.pdf.

Doom, Justin 2014. China supreme court ruling favors AMSC in two Sinovel suits. Bloomberg report, February 19th. www.bloomberg.com/news/articles/2014-02-19/china-supreme-court-ruling-favors-amsc-in-two-sinovel-suits-1-.

Dunker, Robert 2011. Vettel-Team Red Bull wirft McLaren Spionage vor. Newspaper report, April 7th. www.welt.de/sport/formel1/article13103926/Vettel-Team-Red-Bull-wirft-Mc Laren-Spionage-vor.html.

Epoch 2007. www.theepochtimes.com/news/7-7-2/57195.html.

Epoch 2013. Nearly every NYC crime involves cyber, says Manhattan DA. Newspaper report, March 2nd. www.theepochtimes.com/n3/1476827-nearly-every-nyc-crime-involves-cy ber-says-manhattan-da/.

EU 2001. Report on the existence of a global system for the interception of private and commercial communications (ECHELON interception system). www.europarl.europa.eu/sides/getDoc.do?pubRef=-//EP//TEXT+REPORT+A5-2001-0264+0+DOC+XML+V0//EN.

European Lotteries 2017. www.european-lotteries.org/announcement/lotteries-europe-contribute-record-breaking-€-25-billion-society.

Evans 2012. www.telegraph.co.uk/news/uknews/terrorism-in-the-uk/9354373/Cyber-crime-a-global-threat-MI5-head-warns.html.

FAZ 2001. www.faz.net/aktuell/gesellschaft/wirtschaftsspionage-die-europaeer-bestechen-dauernd-die-amerikaner-nie-115502.html.

FAZ 2008. www.faz.net/aktuell/wirtschaft/unternehmen/babyfon-abhoeraffaere-porsche-chef-wiedeking-spielte-den-lockvogel-1538767.html.

FireEye 2012. investors.fireeye.com/releasedetail.cfm?ReleaseID=790574.

FireEye 2016. Redline drawn: China recalculates its use of cyber espionage. www.fireeye.com/content/dam/fireeye-www/current-threats/pdfs/rpt-china-espionage.pdf.

Focus 2012. Magazine report. www.focus.de/reisen/flug/sicherheitsluecken-am-flughafen-berlin-tegel-focus-reporter-dringt-auf-das-rollfeld-vor_aid_858016.html.

Fortune 2001. archive.fortune.com/magazines/fortune/fortune_archive/2001/09/17/310274/index.htm.

Frankel, Glenn 2005. 18 Arrested in Israeli probe of computer espionage. Newspaper report, May 31st. www.washingtonpost.com/wp-dyn/content/article/2005/05/30/AR2005053000486_pf.html.

F-Secure 2013. Sharking: High-rollers in the crosshairs. F-Secure blog post, December 10th. www.f-secure.com/weblog/archives/00002647.html.

FT 2005. Newspaper report. www.ft.com/cms/s/0/2834d598-bc39-11d9-817e-00000e2511c8.html.

FT 2012. Cyber espionage definition. http://lexicon.ft.com/Term?term=cyber-espionage.

Fuld 2001. Study by Fuld&Company, no longer available only.

Gallup 2016. www.gallup.com/businessjournal/188033/worldwide-employee-engagement-crisis.aspx?g_source=employee&g_medium=search&g_campaign=tiles and www.gallup.com/businessjournal/194204/millennials-job-hoppers-not.aspx?g_source=workplace+resignation&g_medium=search&g_campaign=tiles.

GCHQ. www.gchq.gov.uk/what-we-do.

Github 2014. https://github.com/elvanderb/TCP-32764.

Golem 2013. www.golem.de/news/snowden-dokumente-grosse-backbone-betreiber-helfen-geheimdiensten-1308-100753.html.

Google 2010. Blog post, January 12th. http://googleblog.blogspot.de/2010/01/new-app roach-to-china.html.

Google 2014. www.businessinsider.com/google-glass-inventor-it-could-outsource-our-brains-2014-7?IR=T.

Gorman, Siobhan 2012. Chinese hackers suspected in long-term Nortel Breach. Newspaper report, February 14th. http://online.wsj.com/article/SB10001424052970203363504577187502201577054.html.

Greenberg, Andy 2014. The app I used to break into my neighbor's home. www.wired.com/2014/07/keyme-let-me-break-in.

Greenwald 2014. How the NSA tampers with US-made Internet routers. www.theguardian.com/books/2014/may/12/glenn-greenwald-nsa-tampers-us-internet-routers-snowden.

The Guardian 2013. Newspaper report, September 24th. www.theguardian.com/world/2013/sep/24/brazil-president-un-speech-nsa-surveillance.

The Guardian 2014. Newspaper report, July 14th. www.theguardian.com/uk-news/2014/jul/14/gchq-tools-manipulate-online-information-leak.

Hackländer, Friedrich Wilhelm 1846. "Reise in den Orient".

Harris, Shane 2014. Inside the FBI's fight against Chinese cyber-espionage. Magazine article, May 27th. http://foreignpolicy.com/2014/05/27/exclusive-inside-the-fbis-fight-against-chinese-cyber-espionage/.

Heffner, Craig 2013. Exploiting security cameras like a Hollywood hacker. https://media.blackhat.com/us-13/US-13-Heffner-Exploiting-Network-Surveillance-Cameras-Like-A-Hollywood-Hacker-Slides.pdf.

Heise 2004. www.heise.de/ct/artikel/Geld-oder-Netz-289426.html.

Heise 2005. www.heise.de/newsticker/meldung/Drei-Jahre-Haft-fuer-Ericsson-Hacker-150539.html.

Heise 2011. www.heise.de/security/meldung/Allied-Telesis-plappert-geheime-Hintertuer-aus-1251418.html.

Helsingin Sanomat 2006. www.spiegel.de/netzwelt/tech/marken-piraterie-echt-falsche-nokia-handys-a-408270.html.

Henry, Alan 2003. Toyota engineer questioned about Ferrari 'copy'. Newspaper report, November 3rd. www.theguardian.com/sport/2003/nov/03/motorracing.formulaone2003.

History 1966. Based on documentation found on the history channel website. www.history.com/this-day-in-history/auto-safety-crusader-ralph-nader-testifies-before-congress.

Inquirer 2014. www.theinquirer.net/inquirer/news/2349403/evernote-and-deezer-fess-up-to-ddos-attacks.

Internet Live Stats 2016. Internet penetration rate 2016. www.internetlivestats.com.

Investopedia 2017. www.investopedia.com/terms/i/industrial-espionage.asp.

ISAF 2016. ISAF 2016 worldwide shark attack summary. www.floridamuseum.ufl.edu/fish/isaf/worldwide-summary/.

ITPro 2012. Software giants reach financial settlement in long-running corporate theft case. News report, August 3rd. www.itpro.co.uk/642106/sap-agrees-to-306m-oracle-settlement.

Jackson, Kelly 2010. More victims of Chinese hacking attacks come forward. Online report, January 14th. www.darkreading.com/attacks-breaches/more-victims-of-chinese-hacking-attacks-come-forward/d/d-id/1132773.

James, Harold 2012. *Krupp: A History of the Legendary German Firm*. Princeton, NJ: Princeton University Press.

Japan Times 2017. China suspects graduate of Taiwan university of espionage. News report, March 12th. www.japantimes.co.jp/news/2017/03/12/asia-pacific/crime-legal-asia-pacific/china-suspects-graduate-taiwan-university-espionage/#.WSbbLVL5zGI.

Jolly, David 2010. Arrest warrant for Floyd Landis. *New York Times* newspaper report, February 15th. www.nytimes.com/2010/02/16/sports/cycling/16landis.html?_r=0.

Justice 2014. US charges five Chinese military hackers for cyber espionage against U.S. corporations and a labor organization for commercial advantage. US Department of Justice News, May 19th. www.justice.gov/opa/pr/us-charges-five-chinese-military-hackers-cyber-espionage-against-us-corporations-and-labor.

Keromytis, Angelos 2014. From the Aether to the Ethernet – Attacking the Internet using broadcast digital television. Blog post. http://iss.oy.ne.ro/Aether.

Koehler, Thomas 2011. *Social-Media-Management: Chancen der Neuen Medien nutzen – Risiken fuer Unternehmen vermeiden*, IDG, 2011.

Kopplin, Ilka and Karabask, Ina 2011. Technologieklau. Datendiebe im Firmennetzwerk. Magazine article. www.wiwo.de/unternehmen/mittelstand/technologieklau-gefahr-durch-schadsoftware/5752142.html.

KPMG 2016. https://home.kpmg.com/cn/en/home/insights/2016/10/the-13th-fyp-opportunity-analysis-for-chinese-and-foreign-business.html.

Krebs, Brian 2011. Blog post, August 17th. Beware of juice-jacking. http://krebsonsecurity.com/2011/08/beware-of-juice-jacking.

Krebs, Brian 2012. Espionage attacks against Ruskies? Blog post, December 10th. http://krebsonsecurity.com/2012/12/chinese-espionage-attacks-against-ruskies/.

Krebs, Brian 2014. Antivirus is dead: Long live antivirus! Blog post, May 7th. https://krebsonsecurity.com/2014/05/antivirus-is-dead-long-live-antivirus/.

Krupp n.d. www.thyssenkrupp.com/en/company/history/.

Lattmann, Peter 2012. Former Goldman programmer is arrested again. *New York Times* newspaper report, August 9th. http://dealbook.nytimes.com/2012/08/09/ex-goldman-programmer-is-arrested-again.

Leyden, John 2005. Londoners top world in leaving laptops in taxis. www.theregister.co.uk/2005/01/25/taxi_survey.

LFV 2013. Listing based on report found in Franken Manager Magazine, 3–4/13, p. 72.

LinkedIn 2017. www.linkedin.com/pub/brian-shields/8/b43/981 (as of May 24th).

Luxottica 2014. www.luxottica.com/en/luxottica-google-glass.

LVZ 2013. www.presseportal.de/en/pm/amp/6351/2504650.

Maisto, Michelle 2009. Intel study: Stolen laptop cost to businesses $50,000. www.eweek.com/pc-hardware/intel-study-stolen-laptop-cost-to-businesses-50-000.

Manager Magazine 2008. www.manager-magazin.de/finanzen/artikel/a-83614.html.

Markoff, John 2000. Oracle hired a detective agency to investigate Microsoft's allies. New York Times newspaper report. www.nytimes.com/2000/06/28/business/oracle-hired-a-detective-agency-to-investigate-microsoft-s-allies.html.

Markoff, John 2010a. Cyberattack on Google said to hit password system. www.nytimes.com/2010/04/20/technology/20google.html.

Markoff, John 2010b. 2 China schools said to be tied to online attacks. www.nytimes.com/2010/02/19/technology/19china.html.

McAfee 2011. McAfee blog post. http://blogs.mcafee.com/business/global-energy-industry-hit-in-night-dragon-attacks.

Merson, John 1989. *Roads to Xanadu: East and West in the Making of the Modern World*. ABC Enterprises, 1989.

MoscowNews 2013. Russian security agency to buy typewriters to avoid surveillance. News report, July 11th, original source. http://themoscownews.com/russia/20130711/191758523/Russian-security-agency-to-buy-typewriters-to-avoid-surveillance.html, now available via Archive.is http://archive.is/znHFH.

MTV 2014. Nokia paid millions of Euros in ransom. News report, June 17th. www.mtv.fi/uutiset/rikos/artikkeli/nokia-paid-millions-of-euros-in-ransom/3448918.

Mybet 2017. https://help.mybet.com/content/2/21/de/ist-online-wetten-legal.html.

NCPC 2012. www.ncpc.org/resources/files/pdf/internet-safety/13020-Cybercrimes-revSPR.pdf.

Netcraft 2014. Half a million widely trusted websites vulnerable to Heartbleed bug. http://news.netcraft.com/archives/2014/04/08/half-a-million-widely-trusted-websites-vulnerable-to-heartbleed-bug.html.

News in English 2013. Telenor reports industrial espionage. www.newsinenglish.no/2013/03/17/telenor-reports-industrial-espionage.

New York Times 2001. www.nytimes.com/2001/09/07/business/p-g-said-to-agree-to-pay-unilever-10-million-in-spying-case.html

NUE 2017. www.nuernberginfos.de/bedeutende-nuernberger/ulman-stromer.html.

Obama 2015. obamawhitehouse.archives.gov/the-press-office/2015/09/25/fact-sheet-president-xi-jinpings-state-visit-united-states.

ONS 2016. Internet users in the UK: 2016. www.ons.gov.uk/businessindustryandtrade/itandinternetindustry/bulletins/internetusers/2016.

OPENSSL 2014. TLS Heartbeat read overrun. www.openssl.org/news/secadv/20140407.txt.

OSA 1889. Excerpt from the Official Secrets Act of 1889. https://archive.org/stream/41699539073887/41699539073887_djvu.txt.

OVB 2009. Spion aus China in Kolbermoor. Newspaper report, September 4th. www.ovb-online.de/rosenheim/spion-china-kolbermoor-460092.html.

OVB 2013. Newspaper report, March 20th. www.ovb-online.de/muehldorf/spionage-handwerksbetrieben-2810594.html.

Paraszczuk, Joanna 2012. 'Trojan Horse' couple to compensate Novelist. Newspaper report, March 18th. www.jpost.com/National-News/Trojan-Horse-couple-to-compensate-novelist.

Paul, Ryan 2010. Researchers identify command servers behind Google attack. http://arstechnica.com/security/2010/01/researchers-identify-command-servers-behind-google-attack.

Pfaff, Dietmar 2005. *Competitive intelligence in der Praxis. Mit Informationen über Ihre Wettbewerber auf der Überholspur.* Campus.

Point 2004. Old PCs are goldmine for data thieves. www.theregister.co.uk/2004/09/03/old_pcs_not_wiped.

Porter, Michael E. 1980. *Competitive Strategy: Techniques for Analyzing Industries and Competitors.* Free Press.

Poulsen, Kevin. 2014. How Google Map hackers can destroy a business at will. www.wired.com/2014/07/hacking-google-maps.

Proschko, Rudolf. 2012. No title. www.augsburger-allgemeine.de/wirtschaft/Wirtschafts-Spionage-vom-Sofa-aus-id6917026.html.

PWC 2015. Insurance 2020 & beyond: Reaping the dividends of cyber resilience. www.pwc.com/gx/en/insurance/publications/assets/reaping-dividends-cyber-resilience.pdf.

The Register 2017a. LinkedIn U-turns on Bluetooth-enabled 'Tinder for marketers'. www.theregister.co.uk/2017/04/21/linkedin_bluetooth_feature_privacy_concerns/.

The Register 2017b. Dishwasher has directory traversal bug. www.theregister.co.uk/2017/03/26/miele_joins_internetofst_hall_of_shame/.

Reuters 2010. SAP to pay Oracle $1.3 billion in landmark decision. News report. www.reuters.com/article/us-oracle-sap-idUSTRE6AL4IN20101124.

Reuters 2014a. Iranian hackers use fake Facebook accounts to spy on U.S., others. News report, May 29th. www.reuters.com/article/2014/05/29/us-iran-hackers-idUSKBN0E90A220140529.

Reuters 2014b. U.S. may act to keep Chinese hackers out of Def Con hacker event. Reuters News release, May 24th. www.reuters.com/article/us-cybercrime-usa-china-idUSBREA4N07D20140524.

Rubenking, Neil 2012. Industrial espionage worm steals AutoCAD designs, sends to China. Magazine report, June 24th. http://securitywatch.pcmag.com/none/299493-industrial-espionage-worm-steals-autocad-designs-sends-to-china.

Ryan, Thomas 2010. Getting into bed with Robin Sage. Research paper 2010. http://media.blackhat.com/bh-us-10/whitepapers/Ryan/BlackHat-USA-2010-Ryan-Getting-In-Bed-With-Robin-Sage-v10.pdf.

Sahm, Ulrich 2005. Erdbeben in Israels Wirtschaft: Umfassender Spionage-Skandal. TV report, May 30th. www.n-tv.de/politik/dossier/Umfassender-Spionage-Skandal-article151160.html.

Samuel, Henry 2013. BMW accused of spying on low cost electric car Autolib'. Newspaper report, September 10th. www.telegraph.co.uk/motoring/news/10299447/BMW-accused-of-spying-on-low-cost-electric-car-Autolib.html.

Sanger, David 2014. With spy charges, U.S. draws a line that few others recognize. www.nytimes.com/2014/05/20/ rus.us/us-treads- ne-line-in- ghting-chinese-espionage.html.

Securityweek 2014. www.securityweek.com/hackers-attack-shipping-and-logistics-firms-using-malware-laden-handheld-scanners.

Shapiro, Michael J. 2010. Starwood charges that top Hilton execs abetted espionage. Magazine report, January 20th. www.meetings-conventions.com/News/Hotels-and-Resorts/Starwood-Charges-That-Top-Hilton-Execs-Abetted-Espionage.

Sharvit, Noam 2005. YES, Pelephone, Cellcom execs arrested for computer espionage. www.globes.co.il/en/article-918528.

Sharwood, Simon 2013. Don't brew that cuppa! Your kettle could be a spambot. www.thereg ister.co.uk/2013/10/29/dont_brew_that_cuppa_your_kettle_could_be_a_spambot.

ShodanHQ. www.shodanhq.com.

Sicherheitsmelder 2005. www.sicherheitsmelder.de/xhtml/articleview.jsf;jsessionid=38A1B9AC66ADDAF5BF77E0030065E3A7.BoorbergSolrAppLive?id=4602A6C00AA8.htm.

Silk 2008. www.die-seide.de/geschichte-der-seide.

Spiegel 1993. Magazine report: 'Kopiert und gespeichert'. www.spiegel.de/spiegel/print/d-13681478.html.

Spiegel 2013. Magazine report, October 25th. www.spiegel.de/politik/ausland/briten-geheimdienst-gchq-betrieb-wirtschaftsspionage-in-italien-a-929995.html.

Spiegel 2014a. 'A' wie Angela. Magazine report, March 31st. www.spiegel.de/spiegel/print/d-126267965.html.

Spiegel 2014b. www.spiegel.de/netzwelt/web/dlr-mit-trojanern-von-geheimdienst-ausges paeht-a-964099.html.

SST 2017. blog.ssdev.org.

Stern 2007. Newspaper report, April 26th. www.stern.de/wirtschaft/news/industriespio nage-porsche-chef-mit-babyfon-bespitzelt-3089954.html.

Suhl, Sven-Olaf 2006. Diebe stahlen geheime Testkomponenten für Handys. www.heise.de/newsticker/meldung/Diebe-stahlen-geheime-Testkomponenten-fuer-Handys-113993.html.

Supersonic 1998. Transcript of the documentary can be found here. www.pbs.org/wgbh/nova/transcripts/2503supersonic.html.

Symantec 2011. Symantec report, February 2011. www.symantec.com/content/en/us/enterprise/media/security_response/whitepapers/w32_stuxnet_dossier.pdf.

Tagesanzeiger 2014. www.tagesanzeiger.ch/digital/internet/Geheimwaffe-Schreibmaschine/story/14125341?track.

TAZ 2009. Schutz vor Industriespionage. Die Wachstumsbranche. Newspaper report. http://taz.de/Schutz-vor-Industriespionage/!5061818/.

TEA 2010. www.smithsonianmag.com/history/the-great-british-tea-heist-9866709/.

TechAndLaw 2013. Research paper. http://techandlaw.net/security-of-the-digital-natives/.

Tiku, Nitasha 2014. How a hacker intercepted FBI and Secret Service calls with Google Maps. http://valleywag.gawker.com/how-a-hacker-intercepted-fbi-and-secret-service-calls-w-1531334747.

TrapX 2014. www.trapx.com/the-anatomy-of-the-attack.

Trust 2014. Corporate trust studie industriespionage. http://corporate-trust.de/pdf/CT-Studie-2014_DE.pdf.

Tzu, Sun (n.d.)a. *The Art of War*. http://classics.mit.edu/Tzu/artwar.html.

Tzu, Sun (n.d.)b. *The Art of War*. Based on the translation available here. www.strategienet.de/kunst.html.

Tzu, Sun (n.d.)c. *The Art of War*. Based on the translation available here. http://opus.bsz-bw.de/hdms/volltexte/2004/408.

Ulfkotte, Udo 2001. *Wirtschaftsspionage. Wie deutsche Unternehmen von auslän- dischen Geheimdiensten ausgeplündert und ruiniert werden*. Goldmann.

Ulfkotte, Udo 2006. *Der Krieg im Dunkeln*. Eichborn, p. 242.

USAToday 2014. U.S. accuses China of hacking Westinghouse, U.S. Steel. Newspaper report, May 19th. www.usatoday.com/story/news/nation/2014/05/19/us-accuses-china-of-cyber-espionage/9273019/.

VBS. www.vbs.admin.ch/de/themen/nachrichtenbeschaffung/wirtschaftsspionage.html.

VDI 2013. Newspaper report, September 27th. www.vdi-nachrichten.com/Technik-Gesellschaft/Angriffe-im-Netz-intelligenter.

Verfassungsschutz 2014. www.verfassungsschutz.de/de/download-manager/_broschuere-2014-03-spionage-sind-auch-sie-gefaehrdet.pdf.

Verma, Sajal 2014. Searching Shodan for fun and profit. Research paper. www.exploit-db.com/docs/33859.pdf.

Weiss, Joe 2010. *Protecting industrial control systems from electronic threats*. Momentum.

Welt 2007. Newspaper report. www.welt.de/welt_print/article871010/Industriespione-schlagen-immer-oefter-zu.html.

Welt 2013. Die anderen schnüffeln – Deutschland schaut nur zu. Newspaper report, July 6th. www.welt.de/wirtschaft/article117785327/Die-anderen-schnueffeln-Deutschland-schaut-nur-zu.html.

Welt 2014. Newspaper report. www.welt.de/newsticker/dpa_nt/infoline_nt/wirtschaft_nt/ar ticle129841253/Verfassungsschutz-warnt-Wirtschaft-vor-Spionage-aus-China.html.htm.7 and http://edition.cnn.com/2014/05/20/world/asia/china-unit-61398.

Whitney, Lance 2012. Nortel hacked for years but failed to protect itself, report says. www.cnet.com/news/nortel-hacked-for-years-but-failed-to-protect-itself-report-says.

Winkler, Ira 2005. *Spies among us: How to stop the spies, terrorists, hackers, and criminals you don't even know you encounter every day*. Wiley.

Wired 2010a. www.wired.com/2010/01/google-hack-attack/.

Wired 2010b. www.wired.com/2010/07/siemens-scada.

Wired 2017. www.wired.com/story/google-glass-2-is-here/.

WSJ 2009. Computer spies breach Fighter-Jet Project. Newspaper report, April 21st. www.wsj.com/articles/SB124027491029837401head_51yP0Cu1AQGUCs7WAC9ZVN.

WSJ 2014. Hacking: Worse than maritime piracy, not as bad as counterfeiting. Blog post, June 9th. https://blogs.wsj.com/digits/2014/06/09/hacking-worse-than-piracy-not-as-bad-as-counterfeiting/.

Index

Page numbers in bold indicate a table on the corresponding page.

Printed and bound by CPI Group (UK) Ltd, Croydon, CR0 4YY
01/05/2025
01858351-0012